DAN DONOVAN

About the Author

Vera Ryan lectures in Art History at the Crawford College of Art in Cork. She has taught at the National College of Art & Design and was on the board of NCAD and the Irish Museum of Modern Art. Vera has published two volumes of interviews with The Collins Press, *Movers & Shapers: Irish Art since 1960* and *Movers & Shapers 2: Irish Visual Art 1940–2006*.

DAN DONOVAN
An Everyman's Life

VERA RYAN

The Collins Press

Published in 2008 by
The Collins Press
West Link Park
Doughcloyne
Wilton
Cork

and

Everyman Palace Theatre
15 MacCurtain Street
Cork

© Vera Ryan 2008

British Library Cataloguing in Publication Data
Ryan, Vera
Dan Donovan : an Everyman's life
1. Donovan, Dan - Interviews 2. Theatrical producers and directors - Ireland - Biography 3. Theater - Ireland - Cork - History - 20th century 4. Cork (Ireland) - Biography 5. Cork (Ireland) - Intellectual life - 20th century
I. Title II. Everyman Palace Theatre
792'.0233'092

ISBN-13: 978 1 90517 259 7

Typeset by Dominic Carroll
Typeset in Adobe Garamond Pro 11pt/16pt
Printed in Malta

Contents

Photo Credits

Photos pages 2, 17, 39 (top), 144, 155, 161, 163, 167, 168, 174, 180, 186, 188 Private Collection

Photos pages 7, 14, 27, 39 (bottom), 59, 65, 100, 112, 116, 137 no credit

Photo page 10 courtesy of Lauder Brothers

Photos pages 13, 19, 26, 29, 57, 62, 63, 75, 135, 170, 181, 182, 202 by Naomi Daly

Photo page 32 courtesy of Aristo, Cork

Photo pages 38, 44, 73, 86, 145, 148, 158, 160, 197 – Courtesy of *Cork Examiner*

Photo page 40 courtesy of RTÉ

Photo page 55 courtesy of Cork City and County Archives

Photo page 58 by W. Suschitzky

Photo page 66 courtesy of *The Irish Times*

Photo page 81 courtesy of R. W. Hammond, Cork

Photo page 90 photographer unknown

Photos pages 92, 175 courtesy of Irish Press Ltd

Photos pages 125, 128 courtesy of Lensmen

Photo page 138 courtesy of Independent News Ltd

Photo page 147 courtesy of Gaton Photo Studio

Photo page 149 courtesy of *Irish Examiner*

Photo page 177 courtesy of John O'Shea

Photo page 190 by Janice O'Connell, F22

Photo page 192 courtesy of University College Cork

Acknowledgements

The genesis of this book is very much bound up with the Everyman Palace Theatre and I thank everyone there, especially the chairman, Michael White, for gallant support. I thank Dan for so warmly sharing his wonderful memories with me. I particularly thank Pat Talbot, whose initiative and sure-footed advice were core to the whole project. Naomi Daly worked very hard, was thoroughly patient and cordial under pressure and exercised her wide-ranging skills unstintingly for the benefit of the book. Many of the photographs were taken by Naomi. The quest for photographs was helped greatly by many individuals. I thank Lucette Murray, Charlo and Ann Neeson Quain, the Nestor family, John O'Shea, Margaret O'Sullivan, Mary Burrows Pyle, Margaret Burrows Sides and Violet Warner most sincerely. Dan gave us generous access to his own photographic collection.

I also thank the *Irish Examiner*, Independent Newspapers Ltd, The Irish Press Ltd and *The Irish Times*. Ann Kearney at the *Irish Examiner* and Esther Murnane at *The Irish Times* have been most helpful.

My colleagues in the library at the Crawford College of Art & Design provided unfailingly generous support. I extend my sincere gratitude to Martin Hazell, Margaret Kenneally and Fran Moore. I greatly appreciate the support of acting principal, Orla Flynn, and my colleague Dr Julian Campbell.

Cecilia Gallagher, Patricia Lucy, Fr Dermot Lynch, Dr Con Murphy, Canon Murphy-O'Connor PP, Dr Niall O'Doherty, Kevin Olden and Professor Brendan O'Mahony have also been very helpful and I thank them. Last but not least, my warmest thanks go to Willie Smyth, whose advice and support were very generously given throughout. He and my son Tom O'Byrne have brought patience and perception to my role in this project.

Vera Ryan

Foreword

Many of outstanding ability graced the artistic life of Cork in the latter half of the twentieth century. Mention the Cork Film Festival and the name Der Breen springs to mind. Aloys Fleischmann is synonymous with the Choral Festival, James N. Healy with The Southern Theatre Group and John O'Shea with Everyman. The name Seán Ó Tuama will always be associated with Compántas Chorcaí. There hovers, however, at the shoulder of all of these personalities an enduring moral, artistic and intellectual presence. A presence which inspired, anchored and validated much of what was finest in each of the above partnership endeavours. That presence was, and remains, Dan Donovan.

That much-abused term, 'renaissance man', properly applies more to Dan Donovan that to anyone else I've ever known. Actor, director, producer, broadcaster, scriptwriter, cineaste, sailor, follower of the Riverstown Foot Beagles, raconteur, entertainer, critic, teacher, philosopher, historian, the list goes on and on. Here is integrity and breadth of vision in a compassionate, essentially shy and truly humble man. Like moths to a flame, young actors, directors, writers and film-makers of my generation gravitated to Dan's presence. Starved by shallow education systems in the 1960s, here we encountered levels of artistic nurture which blew our minds. For lads like myself and Bob Crowley, Mick McCarthy, Dermot Crowley, Denis McSweeney and a host of others, Dan was our god, we his acolytes.

Many's the time Dan's trusty Renault 4L transported us to rehearsals. Afterwards to partake of refreshment in that den of unbridled bohemianism, 'Healy's Hall' on the South Main Street. Welcome as the refreshment and uplifting as the company invariably was, the Group Theatre was more than just an upstairs room where one drank pints and listened to Dónal O'Donovan warble 'St Louis

Blues'. It was colosseum and senate, forum and circus. It was also our forge. Gathered about Dan, one idea begat another, sparking a third into incandescence. For starters we ate and drank Eisenstein, not to mention Pudovkin. Bergman and Fellini, Stanislavski and Yevtushenko, Ibsen and Chekhov, Pinter and Ayckbourn were all served for main course. Tennessee Williams, Sam Beckett, James Joyce and J. B. Keane did nicely for dessert. Supping with Dan, we believed that we too were demi-gods, specially chosen, blessed with boundless possibilities. In Dan's presence, many felt, myself for the first time, feelings of real empowerment.

It was OK to laugh and to cry. To imagine, to aspire, to hope. We learned it was not just OK to dream. Like breathing, it was essential.

Once I asked Dan how Estragon should feel when delivering a certain line in *Godot*. His answer has remained with me ever since:

'Dredge, boy, dredge.'

Thank you Dan, for sending us out into the world to dredge and to dream.

Go maire tú an céad, a chara.

Pat Butler
Shankill, County Dublin
1 December 2007

Foreword

My first sightings of Dan Donovan were at the crossroads between Evergreen Road and Summerhill South where I lived in the 1950s. Quite a dashing figure he cut astride his BSA motorbike. My earliest encounter with him was when he was drafted in to coach me in my rendering of Pearse's blood-curdling speech over the grave of Ó Donnabháin Rossa at Glasnevin Cemetery. To me, this chap was impressive – even off the motorbike – with his powerful voice and his command of oratory.

We met again when I was transferred from Coláiste Chríost Rí to Presentation College. How lucky to have Dan teach me English. Here was an inspiring teacher, whose instinct was to lead his pupils out into the wide world as per the original meaning of the Latin verb 'educare'/to lead out.

If Glasnevin was the scene of my first stage break, Julius Caesar's Palace in Rome was my next. Dan cast me as Decius Brutus in his top-notch production of Shakespeare's great play. My character is given the vital task of persuading Caesar to come forth and attend the forum. Just one key scene plus a little more later involving fake daggers and pints of Crosse and Blackwell's tomato ketchup, climaxing with 'Et tu, Brute? Then fall Caesar!' Thus was I wafted by Dan into the Major League of Cork theatre at the age of eighteen years.

I had finished up at UCC by 1961 and had started to earn my crust as a young teacher and joyfully rejoined three of the most productive of Cork's theatre groups: Presentation Theatre Guild, still headed by Dan, Ashton Productions under the spirited leadership of Rachel Burrows and Compántas Chorcaí, the Irish language group headed by Dónall Ó Donnabháin leis an t-Ollamh Seán Ó Tuama mar dhramadóir tighis/resident playwright.

There was great fun as we scrimped and scraped. After a while, it became obvious that competition between groups in our small city was cramping each of their styles. Eventually I had approached Dan, Rachel and Seán Ó regarding some cooperation. What emerged was the idea of a coordinated season of six plays to be staged by the various groups. The venue was the cheap-to-rent, dead central Little Theatre in Castle Street. Perfect – except slightly pongy on Fridays because it was sited directly over a fish-shop.

No matter, we were enthusiastic and the umbrella title of Everyman Theatre was chosen. It is taken from a late medieval play which contains the line:

Everyman, I will go with thee and be thy guide.
In thy most need to be at thy side.

The first Everyman season (1963–64) was very successful: the plays were imaginatively done and we were able to keep seat prices low because everyone worked for nothing. The rest of the Everyman story: early (Castle Street), middle (Father Mathew Street), and later (MacCurtain Street) will be unfolded in the pages to come.

Dan is, of course, a natural performer, as a teacher, an actor, a presenter, a raconteur in good company. No better man.

But there is another side. What we came to know was something of the obverse side of the public man – the even more wide-ranging private one. Dan's mind is, quite simply, the finest I have known in my time. Deep, wide and cultured it is. The shelves of his study sag with the weight of his extensive library. All that is best of literature in English and *as Gaeilge*, together with choice translations from the Continent, sit there. When I was last in that room, I noticed that Dan was almost halfway through a biography of the seventeenth century poet, John Donne. At 81 years this might, perhaps, be taken to say it all. But not by a long shot yet.

For in another corner, stacked floor to ceiling are hundreds of records, tapes and CDs, which are regularly played. This I know for certain. For many is the afternoon I have called to his house and there he would be, sitting in his favourite armchair with the westering sun flowing through the window, surrounded by glorious music. My guess is that Dan's musical stash must be one of the most comprehensive private collections of classical recordings in the country. The sweep of it is quite breathtaking – from Medieval music to Renaissance, Baroque to Enlightenment and Romantic to Modern. All musical forms are found here: song and dance, oratorio and opera, choral and chamber music; symphonies and concerti. Astounding stuff.

In May 2006 we celebrated Dan's eightieth birthday. Presentation College renamed its auditorium the Dan Donovan Theatre. In 2007 he received the award for Cork Person of the Year. Dan was genuinely pleased and grateful for all of these plaudits.

But the one that caught him completely by the heart was that which occurred last November at the annual dinner of the Presentation College Union. During his after-dinner speech, the current headmaster, Michael Hennessy, made due mention of Dan's award. Whereupon, the entire company of several hundred men in tuxedo and black tie rose to their feet to give a spontaneous and thunderous ovation for the Dan Donovan they had variously come to know and admire.

Such moments in life cannot be orchestrated. They are exhilarating for those present. How much more so for the recipient … in this case, we shall never know because of the man's inherent modesty. But such moments as these are given only to the rare ones among us. And Dan Donovan is one such rare one.

Go mairir an céad, a chara.

John O'Shea
Nollaig 2007

1

Early Days

When artistic director of Everyman Palace Theatre, Pat Talbot, asked me to interview Dan¹ with a view to publication, I was both honoured and daunted. The story begins just before Dan made his First Communion in the early 1930s.

Vera Ryan

Tell me about your first day with the Presentation Brothers in Cork.

It was sheer chance that I went to Pres as a young boy at all, although my brother Tim had done his Matric and Leaving Cert there in the 1920s. He had been away at Clongowes and my parents decided it would be better to bring him back to Cork to complete his College entrance exams. In those days Pres did Matric in fifth year. A good many tended to leave after fifth year, having secured university entrance. That was the prior history of Pres in my family. My brother had a good reputation because he was a very skilled rugby player and secured several inter-provincial caps for Munster.

There was an intention that Tim would do medicine. He did medicine but he took rather a time at it. I presume the seeds of medicine were developed through contact with my Aunt Lell's dispensary in the old maternal family house in the West Village in Ballincollig, where there was constant talk about medical matters and

Aunt Lell.

regular contact with Doctors Harding and Crowley. Lell was always talking about patients' ailments. She adored Dr Harding. After the Great Flu of 1918, Dr Harding's only loss among his patients was one of the Chalky Mahonys in the old Powder Mills, a youngish man with a big family. Dr Harding was very upset over that. All the weaklings wriggled through and survived. He was followed by Dr Crowley, who was nicknamed Candy. By virtue of being in the dispensary Lell was also in contact with the relieving officer of the area. Because of her efforts through Billy Kenefick, the relieving officer, to get a few shillings for them, we knew the names of almost everybody in the area who was in distress, and there were many. Sums ranged from as low as half a crown a week to larger sums where there was greater necessity. The relieving officer had to monitor that very limited scheme. It was very primitive but it did help out enormously. Its inadequacies were obvious. A good deal of the work on the ground was done by Lell on her 'High Nelly' bicycle. She was extremely friendly with the Kenefick family and when she became old and ill, Dr Paul Kenefick, a relative of Billy, looked after her treatment.

I entered Pres private junior school in 1932 after a false start in Ballincollig. Were it not for a lady teacher in Boys' Infants I might have had to postpone the Pres experience until much later. As a four-and-a-half year old I somehow got into difficulties with a female teacher, whose name remains engraved on my memory. Unfortunately, because teachers were involved, as a very small fellow, I became a source of conflict between my mother, who was principal of the Girls' School in Ballincollig, and the head of the Boys' School in Ballincollig. The impasse was solved by a family decision to send me to Pres where my brother had been happy and successful.

Was corporal punishment involved?

Corporal punishment was involved, which led to me having nightmares and disturbing the whole family. But the situation was really exasperated by the principal of the Boys' School reporting my absence from school to the local sergeant. I think there was an obligation to do so, but it was an officious act and it led to my departure to Pres. I was six when I entered Pres. I had a purple blazer and a purple cap; that was the sum total of the Pres uniform. Pa Joe Ahern, later a well-known dentist in Cork and attending Pres at the time, took my hand, brought me on the bus and looked after me until I found my feet. The Aherns were a particularly nice family. One of Pa Joe's older brothers, Tim, a man with a bit of a physical disability, was a great friend of the family. We knew him well because he was in charge of the library which was across the road from our house on Station Road. He was part of my early introduction to masses of books. We had a great day when the County Council library van came to change the book stock.

One of the first tasks that I had was to be trained for my First Communion. That aspect of my upbringing was neglected due to the Ballincollig impasse. In a group of three or four we were inducted into the old green catechism under the tender care of Brother Loyola,

'Lolly', an extremely kind and practical man who was in charge of the Junior School. You might be interrupted in the catechism class by the sale of a school cap to someone. His tiny office off the Physics Room on Western Road contained great boxes of caps, scarves and blazers. He bought them from the makers or shops and organised the distribution in school.

Teaching was very sympathetically done in Pres. I remember being brought down to a very kindly Fr Anthony in the nearby old St Francis church on Liberty Street for my First Confession. It was the church of the old marsh in a very poor area of Cork. In a peculiarly honest way the old church reflected the simple, spiritual Franciscan ethos. This is not evident to me in the monstrous, Byzantine, impersonal and garish church that replaced it in the 1950s, indicative of all that has gone wrong with a Christianity which reflects the imperial rule of Constantine. I had none of the experiences related by Frank O'Connor in *First Confession*. I had the usual sins: I had been disobedient, said bad words and so on. I made my Communion on a Saturday morning all on my own in Ballincollig Parish Church with the curate, Fr Ahern, officiating. All the family were there. We spent the day in Cork visiting Thompson's Restaurant in Princes Street and going to the pictures.

So you settled into the school?

I settled rapidly into the routine in Pres. When I started, the classes were open in the old method, in the main building. There were three or four classes going on in the great stretch of space on the upper storey of the school. Very shortly though, by the time I was in second class, partitions were installed so that each class had a room to itself. As soon as the individual rooms came, I think the quality of attention and education were better.

The school bought the first of two Georgian houses on the

Mardyke. A tree from the garden formed a seat in the yard for a long time. The buying of the field across the road enabled and extended rugby training and other recreational facilities. The present school now stands on this field. The Brothers bought the place out in Bishopstown for sports facilities in 1961, before a decision was made to build on this field. In those early days we had our sports days and training in the field behind Mardyke House bordering the river, where the Brothers lived. They have a cultural centre there nowadays. They had that house since 1921. The six or seven Brothers who were directly involved with the school lived there and the grounds were thoroughly used for sports and training. It was really an extension of the school. The mill stream ran at the side of the Mardyke and had been directed from the Lee at the weir further up, above Mardyke House, as part of the general industrial development in the nineteenth century to power the Beamish Maltings.

The yard space increased, our playground was expanded and the through-entrance past the bicycle sheds from Western Road to Mardyke was developed. In a short time when the weather became good, from September to early November and from April to June, as regularly as possible, I cycled in from our house in Ballincollig. It would be about five miles. Luckily the Straight Road was built at the time so it was a relatively easy inward journey. On the way home I used to race the old tram, the 'Muskerry Dasher'. I was always sure of catching up with it when it stopped at Carrigrohane Station, where we parted company as it headed to Blarney and I to my home.

My aunt Lell introduced me to bicycling by buying me my first bike from a solicitor who was a neighbour of hers, Gardiner Wallace. His son Aubrey changed bikes and I got Aubrey's, bought for the noble sum of ten bob. My second aunt, Kit in Cork, bought me my first full Hercules bike, of which I was so proud, when I was about thirteen. Kit was the youngest of the Cody aunts. My mother

[Christine] came between her and Lell. Lell was always on her bicycle. When I think of a 'High Nelly' I think of Lell perched on the saddle and always heading somewhere. I think the second of the Georgian street houses purchased rather later by the Order was owned by a Mrs O'Donovan. Coincidentally my aunt Kit had a flat there. When we were living in Ballincollig I had the run of the flat, especially at exam times. I could let myself in and make a snack or my aunt would leave something for me.

I made my Confirmation under the loving tutelage of Brother Carthage. One of my greatest memories of that was an excursion for the whole Confirmation class to Youghal, by train, with Carthage ensuring none of us got lost or drowned or wet.

I'm quite sure I was very happy in Pres Junior School, a happiness that continued for the rest of my school days. There was little or no punishment. You might get a crack across the legs occasionally. But the general atmosphere was benign. Authority wasn't exercised as a tyranny. The private junior school was later closed. The last sixth class was accommodated in the new building and at the end of 1986, the old fee-paying junior school ceased to exist.

The next step for me was the rather more serious business of entering the secondary department of Pres. It meant meeting an enormous number of new pupils entering Pres for the first time. They would come from national schools around the city, including from St Joseph's Primary School, which adjoined Mardyke House on the east side and was, and is of course, run by the Brothers. Anyone from St Joseph's, all other things being equal, would be entitled to enter Pres secondary. A number of able students would get a scholarship.

What were the criteria for entering Pres secondary school?

There was an entrance exam, limited to three subjects: Irish, English and Maths. It was reasonably tough. Very important was the tradition of family attendance. An elder brother or father could pave the way. Another criterion would be the accommodation of new arrivals in Cork. Unusually, the school had a good record for keeping an open house. Many of the sons of the Jewish community in Cork would have been fellow classmates of my own. Over a period of several years many of the leading Jews in Cork were educated in Pres. It was sad in a way seeing so many later leaving Ireland and even going as far as Israel in pursuance of their professional careers. The Schers, the Slesses, the Newmans, the Moseleys, the Goldbergs and others participated fully in the school's ethos. Many made enormous contributions. For instance, David Marcus's work as a writer and anthologist is notable.

It wasn't always easy going for the Jewish community. There was one period when a certain Superior imposed a ban on Jewish boys which lasted a couple of years, though I don't think it affected any pupils at the school at the time. Wiser counsels rapidly prevailed and the situation returned to normal very quickly. I think it involved a

Presentation College, Western Road, Cork c. *1950.*

law case in which a young Brother was accused of excessive physical punishment on a young student in the South Mon [South Monastery] – not a Jew – in which Gerald Goldberg undertook the case for the client family, leading to a reaction which was over the top. Gerald Goldberg, one of the leading men in the cultural life of Cork, a great patron of the arts and a Lord Mayor in 1977, was a great admirer of Pres principals: Dr Connolly, known as 'the Man', and at a later time of Brother Jerome, founder of the SHARE (Students Harness Aid for the Relief of the Elderly) organisation. SHARE was designed to involve Pres boys seriously in social work, in this case with the providing of accommodation and care for the lonely elderly living in inadequate conditions in the area. The principle of care was always emphasised in school life. I was involved in the school committee of St Vincent de Paul, visiting the needy and distributing food and clothing around the heavily populated area adjoining the school to the east.

Pres Junior School was largely taught by Brothers but now in secondary there was the introduction to a large group of lay teachers, who were one of the strengths of the school, as most of them stayed and gave continuity and a sense of security. It was fairly highly organised.

I suppose team sports were very important?

They were. Very soon I was playing games regularly and it wasn't long before I was training for the Cork and Munster Junior Rugby cups. The great trainer we had was a man who belonged to a family very much at the heart of Pres sport, a man called Pat Barry. His brother Des also trained Pres cup teams. Sadly, Pat died in harness. He dropped dead of a heart attack while the team he trained was playing at a match in Limerick. I was at the match and I can still recall the horror around the ground and afterwards at the hotel where the team were, when the news came through that Pat had passed away.

In the early years up to and after the First World War, Pres had been a rugby and hurling school. There is a photo of Bill Twomey, who took over as manager of the Opera House in the 1950s, holding his hurley while a pupil in Pres. There was a Brother in Pres, a Brother Dermot whom Tim knew well, who taught hurling there and fell foul of the Gaelic Athletic Association [GAA] through some administrative pettifogging. He got so annoyed and upset that he withdrew the Pres team from the hurling competitions sometime early in the 1920s.

For class reasons – the strength of the middle class from whom they were drawing their pupils – both Pres and Christians in Sydney Place were rugby schools. The approach of the Brothers in both Pres and Christians would, I think, have been pragmatic. Hurling would have belonged to the North Monastery, a splendid Christian Brothers school where Jack Lynch was a pupil. Frank O'Connor, Michael O'Donovan as he then was, went to the Mon for a time. As did Seán Ó Ríordáin. It was the biggest school in Cork for a long time. Hurling belonged also in Farranferris, the seminary which drew its students from the entire diocesan area; many of whom might have been expected to go to Maynooth to become priests. Farranferris was the school attended by Aloys Fleischmann and Seán Ó Riada,[2] our great musicians.

Many years later, in the 1960s, I discussed the GAA ban on playing 'foreign games' like rugby with Fr Cormac MacCarthaigh. He was very stuck into the GAA. He said he believed that variety was the spice of life but that it was better that schools specialised. Big team games could be mighty expensive and maybe one major sport was perhaps enough for any one school.

Was the teaching good?

Pres had a very good teaching reputation. I have wonderful memories of my teachers, especially Connie Buckley, nicknamed 'Pug', who was a superlative teacher of Irish and English and who left a great

Mr & Mrs Donovan's honeymoon photograph c. *1910.*

mark on me. We were quite quickly immersed in studying for the Inter Cert. The 'powers that be' in the school always liked to keep the academic prowess of the college to the fore by winning government scholarships at the Inter Cert level. There were two grades, £40 and £80. I repeated Inter Cert to get one. I went near it but didn't get it. My hopes of adding my name to the distinguished list of scholarship holders didn't materialise then.

Unfortunately my mother died that year, 1941. My father had already died in 1935. So I became 'Mrs Donovan's orphan boy'.

Did the fact that you felt secure in Pres help you through this time?

It certainly did. It bridged the thing psychologically for me. There was great support from the school. I vividly remember two of the Brothers, Brother Liguori and Brother Alban, coming out to my mother's funeral. The way we dealt with all that was, I suppose, quite stoical.

Was Pres a bit less austere than its rival schools in the city?

We realised we were in a way privileged at Pres.

The fees were rather small, a couple of guineas, nothing exorbitant. Lots of people sent their sons there. I suppose it was elitist to a degree, without being obtrusively so.

Our great rival as a fee-paying school was the Christian Brothers school in Sydney Place. That traditional rivalry reached fever point during the Munster Cup rugby competitions. The ethos in Christians would be much same as in Pres. There would have been a more liberal regime in Sydney Place than would be expected in other Christian Brother schools, on the basis that they were dealing with the upper crust of the city. To us, the regime for the Pres Brothers seemed more kind and sympathetic to the human needs of its own members. At least, so it seemed to us.

What were the friendship patterns?

Friendships did develop between boys from both schools but there were strong family loyalties to both educational establishments. There would be bitterness where parents who had been past pupils would send their children to the rival school. This would have been caused maybe by a bit of family dissent where mothers and fathers would have different traditions. The mother would occasionally insist: 'There is no way I am letting him go to that place. All my brothers went to Christians/Pres' as the case might be. It usually depended on the power of the mother or the father in the house. Such changes of loyalty were not uncommon but the basic loyalties were very consistent.

Schools were of course segregated. Our nearest female rival just across the river was the girls' school, St Aloysius's, where my sisters Patty and Betty went. The budding romances in Pres would tend to have been associated with St Al's, whereas the boys in Sydney Place would be drawn to St Angela's. Culture with a capital K wouldn't have been a great part of the curriculum of either Pres or Christians until later.

Could you explain the expansion of Catholic secondary schools in Ireland, in the period prior to the introduction of free education in the late 1960s?

When general education came for Catholics in the late nineteenth century, orders like the Pres Brothers jumped in and availed of the possibilities. The development of all the teaching orders expanded enormously. The basic movement was to provide education for the masses of young people from poorer families. To some degree Pres and Christians in Sydney Place were catering for a class, the middle class, which had already achieved prosperity. But both schools strengthened and widened that prosperity.

Pres used sometimes be called a 'garrison' school in the early days. 'Garrison' was an insult hurled at Pres because of its collaboration with what was viewed by some of the ordinary citizens as an English

Mrs Donovan's certificate (detail), 1930.

ethos in education. There was a perception that they were *ag rith i ndiaidh na n'uaisle*, in a trot after the grandees. That was a phrase used to observe a snobbery where people got above their fellow citizens. The real motive was to move the middle and lower class Catholics into competition for better employment in the professional and business life of Cork.

When I hear you use a phrase like 'ag rith in ndiaidh na n'uaisle' *it makes me wonder do you sometimes think in Irish?*

I suppose I was influenced to some degree by a house that was very Irish. My mother of course had to learn Irish as a teacher and she learned it well. She had to knuckle down and learn it at the time of the political changeover in the 1920s. She loved Irish.

On the other hand my father grew up in a large household in Glandore and he belonged to that bridge generation where parents and elders never used Irish to a child at all because the children were destined to go away to earn a living. He and my uncle Dinny were trained in the National School and at home to learn English in order to pass the entrance exams to the Royal Irish Constabulary, the RIC. Their father had been married twice and there was a big family of sons. They had to get out of the 33½ acres and small farmhouse which still remain with my relatives. My father, who was born in 1870, spoke half Irish. Half his vocabulary was Irish but I have no sense listening back that he had any feeling for the structure of the Irish language. For instance referring to one of my mother's cousins he'd say 'Oh she's the deep *ciúin ciúntach*', meaning 'she's quiet and it's a furtive quietness.' 'Here's the *beanín mallaithe* [troublesome, interfering, little woman]', he'd say about a troublesome female relation arriving. When I remember these phrases which he used I now recognise the grammatical accuracy. *Ín* is a diminutive and masculine by grammar in Irish. All diminutives are masculine in Irish. Here he was using Irish, pronouncing and using it accurately but I don't think he had the run of an Irish sentence, coming from a background that was intensely Irish but where spoken Irish was lost in that generation.

Through my background I was very aware of the rural scene. As

The Donovan Family c. 1921. l–r: *Mrs Donovan, Patty, Mr Donovan holding Betty, Tim & cousin Lena.*

my father came from the depths of a rural Gaeltacht there was a sense of diverse origins in the family. We were at home in both the country and the city but I think we maintained a good deal of country values.

During the Troubles, when Betty was a babe in arms, and before I was born, two of my father's nephews, Danilo and Tim – strong family names – were involved in the Kilmichael ambush on the Irish side. My father had by this time retired from the RIC.

They were on the run and Danilo, who was my father's favourite nephew, was concealed in our teacher's residence in Ballincollig for a fortnight until the heat was off, thus illustrating the eternal truth that blood is thicker than water. Despite my mother's very strong anxiety, justice was done to Danilo on the run. It was a brave act for my father to show this family loyalty because of his own former employment in the old British police system. As a teacher in the local school my mother would have also been expected to be very conformist. No one in Ballincollig who might have been expected to know about this said anything.

The Cavalry Barracks was burnt to the ground in those years and many goods were looted. Lell bought an excellent portable military bookcase from one of the looters. It remains in my possession. She got it for the knock-down price of ten bob. There was no middle man so all the profit was the looter's. She used to be taunted by a neighbour about having a bit of furniture looted from the Barracks. The Irish army came back to the Barracks during the Second World War, after it was rebuilt.

Your mother continued teaching in Ballincollig right up to and during the War?

Yes. My mother died in harness as they say. I remember in my mother's latter days when I came home from Pres, I'd go across to the old school, where she'd be at her desk correcting copies, to bring her home for dinner. The school was the old Ballincollig pre-Catholic Emancipation church. It was a pretty dire building but morale was high. I'd watch the rats while I was waiting. I remember one very well, a very well-filled, contented one who would come out from a hole in the wall. My mother would stamp her foot and he'd go back in. The Boys' School had the main nave in front and the Girls' School was at the back. There was the main space, maybe the aisle, where my mother would teach fourth to sixth class. She had very nice colleagues, Mrs O'Neill and Miss O'Neill, no relation, who looked after the infants. I was intrigued as a child by the fact that Miss O'Neill was one of the first people I knew who drove a Baby Austin car.

The family home was across the road from the school on Station Road in one of the three houses reserved by the parish for the teachers in the school. My father did the cooking and grew the vegetables until he died aged 65. When my father died, after the morning dispensary sessions in which Lell would help out were over, she'd come up and look after us. The meal would be in the late afternoon of necessity. Nearly always when my mother came in from school, she'd sit down to the piano and play music. There was a huge mass of sheet music in the house. It was salon music. My aunt Kit and my mother often sang and played music. One of the last nights before my mother died the two of them, alto and soprano, sang a duet, *Flow on, Thou Shining River* by Tom Moore.

Patty played but not very well. She wouldn't like to hear me say that. Neither Betty nor I played. I had a good ear but I never succeeded in getting my two hands to combine. I could play out a tune in treble. Getting our first battery radio set was a huge thing – that happened shortly after my father died. We invested in the radio set. Ever after that there was music and drama. I was a great fan of the Radio Éireann players and great actors like Michael Dolan. Sunday evenings had the big productions and they went on all during the War and well into the 1960s.

Despite the early deaths of my parents, the enormous generosity of the women in my family who rallied round and helped both in terms of finance and support made it possible to feel secure. For instance this house I live in here in Turner's Cross was first rented, and later bought, to deal with the situation that arose from the deaths of my mother and father during my youth. I

Dan in a toy car c. 1930.

think one of the most important aspects was the sense of mental and physical security I had from them at a time of threat and uncertainty. My aunt Kit rented the house from Dr Gerry Murphy. He had taken it over from the Corporation as an investment after the builder went bankrupt during its construction in the early 1930s. We paid 25 or 30 bob a week rent. It kept us together: my aunt Kit, my brother Tim who was finishing his medical degree in UCC at the time, myself, Betty and, during the holidays, Patty.

Patty in Dunmanway helped the family here. She was employed in the girls' secondary school, Maria Immaculata, and eventually became vice-principal. She had tremendous practical skills. I still use the pullovers that she knitted for me. I still don't have to buy a sock. She died in 1996 aged 84. She knitted constantly and enthusiastically and practised all kinds of needlework. She had a flat in Dunmanway and spent a great part of her school holidays here and in her beloved Youghal. She was a powerful strength to us. She'd arrive home at

Christmas laden with goods from Atkins in Dunmanway. She used to travel by train but when I eventually acquired a second-hand Ford – around 1958 – I'd go down and collect her and all the goods.

Turner's Cross was probably very different then to the old garrison village of Ballincollig.

Turner's Cross was an expanding area in the 1930s. The great American-designed,[3] recently built, concrete church of Christ the King [1931] was and remains an unusual and compelling piece of architecture with its great cantilevered roof, wide spaces and striking image of Christ the King. With the material of its construction it reminded us poignantly of the changes that occurred leaving Séamus Murphy's 'stonies' virtually deprived of their craft of stone cutting, especially in ecclesiastical architecture.[4] The challenge for the builder was enormous. The budget of £20,000 was exceeded by £10,000. The unfortunate man died soon after. Every precious thing has a price. This is the church I have worshipped in all my life. But when we came here in 1941 it was a chapel of ease for the South Parish. It didn't become a full parish church until Bishop Lucey –sometime in the 1960s or 1970s – re-organised the parish system of the diocese. I remember my aunt paying dues to Canon Mc Sweeney from Douglas in whose parish we were, despite being 100 yards from Christ the King.

These houses are a fairly distinctive group of similar box-like detached houses, just at the start of Curragh Road and opposite the Turner's Cross football stadium in all its various names. We moved into the house in July or August of 1941. I think I still have the Nat Ross bill for transporting us from Station Road. My first impressions of this house were the giant stacks of turf brought in by rail as wartime fuel to the area behind the house now occupied by Mercier Park. We were not short of wet turf. We had that and 'the glimmer', the weak gas supply available a few hours a day in strict wartime rationing. The train line from Macroom to Capwell Bus Station ran behind the houses, bringing not only turf to us but petrol for the buses. I later liked the fact that there was a previous tenant, Ettie Jenkins, who was a great member of the Cork Operatic Society and that James N. Healy was born in a small house across the road. I thought of it as having a long theatrical history. We rented for many years until I became

Christ the King Church, Turner's Cross, Cork, 2007.

settled in my teaching career and had the wherewithal to purchase the house at a reasonable rent, as a sitting tenant.

You were so fortunate to have those wonderful aunts.

I often think with awe of the wonderful women of that older genera-tion. In addition to that, the particular families, the Codys and the Barretts, had many daughters. They went back a century in educa-tion in Ballincollig. I think my great grandfather Barrett had a hedge school starting out. Hence a very strong tradition in teaching and education. Hence also a robust and independent spirit. That was enriched by marriage to both teachers and police. For instance one grand-aunt who had been trained in Alexandra College in Dublin married Jack Murphy from Duhallow, who became headmaster of the Boys' School in Ballincollig. I think he was a widower when he married my grand-aunt. My grand-aunt was assistant in the Girls' School and when the vacancy for headmistress arose, the parish priest felt that since she had been trained at a Protestant training college, it was inappropriate for her to be headmistress of the Girls' School. That would be back in the 1880s or 1890s.

As a small boy, I had certain days for going down to their lovely house in East Village, with its fine bay windows. For a time after my father's death, we stayed with our cousins there.

How do you remember Cork city in your youth?

Cork was socially a bit mixed in the 1930s and 1940s because of Ford's Factory and the various woollen mills. I think the middle classes were strong enough. It was probably above average in prosperity but there were great pockets of poverty. As I was growing up these pockets of poverty were being alleviated by the benevolent and successful housing schemes in places like Gurranebraher and all the way up from the North Cathedral to the new 'red city', as it was called. You could see all the expansion behind Pres, all the red roofs going on the buildings. Further successful housing schemes were built in Ballyphehane near where I live. All that meant the clearing out of the unhygienic laneways and slums that characterised the older city.

What was your first introduction to opera?

I went to my first opera which was *Faust* with the Dublin Grand Opera Society [DGOS], coming in by bus from Ballincollig in about 1939–40. There were great encores and when we got back to the bus office late for the eleven o'clock bus, it was gone. There were five or six other people from the Opera House. A kind inspector calmly called a bus that had turned in and was reporting to the offices on 42 Grand Parade – situated where Pres had been before moving to

Western Road in the later nineteenth century – and asked would the driver ever drop these people out to Ballincollig. And at about twenty past eleven a full, old, red Irish Omnibus Company [IOC] bus drove out the Straight Road and got us home safely. It was an extraordinary kind of personalised service, a very good old service. The passenger train to Ballincollig had stopped by this time. Because it was a garrison town with huge cavalry barracks there, you had the train. The old 'Muskerry Dasher' was really only a mile from Ballincollig. The Bandon line was only up the hill. The infrastructure had been very good, maybe for military reasons. But by the 1940s the buses had more or less replaced the train, which carried on, on a commercial basis, especially for Macroom Fair Days, but ceased to carry passengers.

Patty used to come into school by train, and walk up from the Bandon line terminal opposite City Hall to Sharman Crawford Street. Betty came in by bus. I was going to Cork pretty regularly before I was living in Cork at all. I used to be brought in every Saturday when my mother was still going strong. We used to be brought in to the matinee in the Opera House if there was one. My mother was partial to a decent Wild Western, a horse opera as they were called. I can recall things like John Ford's *Stage Coach* from quite an early age. We'd go to one or the other, cinema or theatre depending on the choice available. But certainly to the matinee at the Opera House, especially when the Clopet–Yorke theatre company began to do summer seasons in the mid 1930s.

Did the visiting theatre groups affect the ordinary daily atmosphere of the city?

Cork like all the big centres had theatrical digs. O'Faolain's mother took in 'theatricals' as they were called. She supplemented her husband's income and pension from the RIC. O'Faolain writes quite vividly about the comings and goings and the atmosphere these rather exotic people brought to what was a rather homely house in Half Moon Street, near the Opera House. He tells us in his autobiography *Vive Moi!* (1964) about being sent up to the Railway Station to spot any lonely-looking theatricals and bring them down to his mother. His mother, Mrs Whelan, became known to Betty as she served her time in the pharmacy in Castle Street. She was always talking about Sean. You'd get all the news about him in an effusive account. She was full of mother's pride. Theatricals would stay near the Opera House if they could. I think they spread out afterwards, to where their 'bush telegraph' spread the news of good digs.

The advent of a regular repertory company made a huge difference to the continuity of the Opera House. In the early 1930s, I think the Opera House would close for the summer but then in the later 1930s, it remained open. During the summer great actors would go to less important centres than London. In 1938 Peggy Ramsay, the great agent afterwards in London when she had every big name on her books, played in the Cork Opera House. Playing in the Opera House in that year also, the name of one of the detective plays put on there, *The Amazing Dr Clitterhouse,* stands out in my memory. There are lots of huge names; for example Sir John Martin Harvey during the summer of 1939 performed his set piece, *The Burgomaster of Stillemonde,* in Cork. Clopet always had his eye out for big names, as he probably did some agency work as well. Because of Clopet's sharpness he would always succeed in getting someone who was resting. The Clopet–Yorke company had usually a week or fortnight's run, during which they rehearsed the next play and planned the next production. They did use shortcuts quite often. Clopet was extremely industrious and the productions as I remember them were extremely efficient, very often excellent.

It was John Daly during the War who succeeded in keeping

the Opera House going, by also encouraging and developing local companies.

Where would the Donovan family shop?

In the Ballincollig days, we shopped for groceries and fuel in John Boyd's store on Main Street. This was a very user-friendly shop. We had our little book, in which the items were listed, and duly paid up when my mother got her monthly cheque. In practice it meant that no member of the family was ever short of anything. But we always bought our clothes in Roche's Stores on Patrick Street [Saint Patrick's Street] in Cork, where the head of the menswear department was the senior Mr Ben Dunne. I think we followed him when he set up his own business across the road. I remember being brought into him for sundry items and remarking on his strong Northern accent. He was extremely attentive and pleasant, and would always remember my mother. He dealt with us, his reliable customers, in a very personal way, even though he lacked the appropriate Cork accent.

I taught his two sons many years later, Ben and Frank. They were devoted to work and horses. Frank I remember as a youngster attending numerous gymkhanas and horse shows. They were very pleasant boys causing no bother, not very interested in the academic world. When their father went out on his own, they worked a great deal to help. They were a strongly industrious family and they threw their weight behind the family developments in the retailing line.

Tell me about Der Breen, the great Film Festival man and your friendship with the whole Breen family.

Der came I suppose late-ish into my life. When I came in to Turner's Cross after my parents were both dead, I met Der for the first time. The Breens had come up from Waterford and had settled in Cork. We were about to undertake our Leaving Cert. I suppose I was rather lonely and confused at the time. I was still trying to find my feet in Cork, becoming a little city boy rather than someone cycling or going by bus five miles out to Ballincollig. I was going from a small village and coming into the big smoke. Der and I became extremely friendly. We had somehow or another a common interest in the theatre and doing plays.

Der's mother, Ciss, was a very quiet, gentle, sympathetic woman. The Breens lived in 'Alverna' in the rectangular enclave of homes near Pres. O heavens, I was really able to use that house almost as my own. It was kind of a home from home. She really in a sense took the place of something of the mother and father that I lost. It was a wonderfully hospitable, warm house. The piano was always playing. There was always music in that house. It was a great base and centre for me and an extension to my own family who were also extremely protective. I was broadening out my interests and my feelings were broadening out through the warm friendship and hospitality of the Breen family. The dad was a very nice man, a quiet man with a strong Waterford accent, a tall, thin, grey-haired man, very warm again. I think he was in CIÉ [Córas Iompair Éireann] on the administration side. He may have done insurance as well. He didn't interfere. Both he and she were very un-interfering, which is the best way I could put it. They were delighted to see things going on. They had come to Cork as well, you see. I suppose they were in the same way working their way into a new environment. Certainly I am eternally grateful for all their warmth and for all their hospitality, at the time I needed it.

In one sense leaving Ballincollig and coming to live in Cork after my mother's death increased my possibilities. First of all I could go to the theatre any time and secondly Der and I had the idea of doing a couple of school plays. I remember our first effort: a typical kind of frustrated effort, a play by a Cork playwright, John Bernard

McCarthy. It was a very broad comedy called *Cough Water*. I think maybe there were two glorified rehearsal performances done in the school, but it never got a proper production. We were fiddling away at it for about a year; that would be about 1942–3.

Where would you go to have a snack when you weren't at home or in the Breen's?

There was a little Italian restaurant down the Western Road a couple of hundred yards from the school, called Macari's. They had ice cream and coffee. One of the boys attended the school in fact. They were extremely warm-hearted people too. Their prices, thinking back on them, were appallingly cheap: four pence and six pence for a cup of coffee. They had tea, buns and delicious ice cream that they made themselves. It was a great port of call and a kind of a trough for our casual eating in those days. You'd get tea and buns and milk and so on.

Pres also had a little cafeteria, run by a rather tenacious but really nice man called Denis and later by Bill Hannon. You'd get tea and buns and milk there at any time. I remember Brother Austin was a bit fastidious and he felt the cafeteria did not conform to the highest of hygiene standards. Denis also looked after the heating boilers! And Brother Austin, probably an environmentalist before his time, felt that the systems as it were of the café weren't quite as good as they should be. He was always campaigning for improvements. If you went in for a bun or something, Denis, who had a bald head and peaked cap, might take the cap off and hit you over the head and say 'you owe me sixpence!' He operated a little credit system. So you didn't starve if you didn't have the penny or two pence for a doughnut or cheesecake or a ring or bit of 'donkey's gudge', as he'd call a rather thick slab cake. He had all these cakes supplied by Ormond and Ahern's Bakery. I'm sure the amount of lard in all of them wouldn't be recommended by a dietitian today. It certainly fed us well and there was always food available at a very cheap price.

Tell me about the Father Mathew Hall where you put on some school plays.

It is a Capuchin hall, next to Holy Trinity Church. It opened in 1907. *The Capuchin Annual* came out each year from 1930 to 1977 as rather a prestigious publication.[5] There was a genuine cultural involvement from the Order in those days when there wasn't too much encouragement from many sources. Quite a few groups like the Lee Players and the Father Mathew Players acted there. It was a club, with a billiard room, a reading room and space for other activities. A man there called Gerry O'Mahony did a great deal of work and gave us help when we were starting out with our play. Brendan Breen, Der's brother, had been for some years training as a Capuchin priest, and had come out but maintained close contact with the Order. The Breens in general seemed well in with the Capuchins and the Father Mathew Hall.

Father Mathew Hall, Father Mathew Street, Cork, 2007.

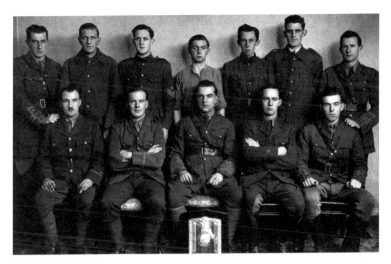

Presentation College Union, 1946. Cast of Journey's End. *Front row l–r:
D. Coughlan, D. Donovan, D. Breen, J. Daly, R. Burke. Back row l–r: T. Weldon,
T. Stack, B. Pierce, D. Coughlan, F. Kelleher, M. Pierce, C. Roche.*

Were the drama festivals taking off when you were at secondary school?

The drama festivals suddenly became all the thing. During the War, I
suppose people were making their own entertainment, because there
was little coming in from abroad. We were isolated. Here then were
competitions developing all over the country; every place was doing
plays, from the remotest country village to the cities. We all got
caught up in it. There were excellent adjudicators, who I must say in
general, not true of all of them, but in general gave both their time
and their patience and their teaching skills to people who they felt
were seriously tackling plays. J. J. Henry, Gabriel Fallon the critic in
the *Irish Standard* and lots of people from Dublin, including Mícheál
Mac Liammóir, Lennox Robinson, Shelah Richards – wife of playwright Denis Johnston – and Ria Mooney came around and gave
their help and of course their prestige to the festivals.

Journey's End marked our first entry as Presentation Theatre

Guild [PTG] to the first Drama Festival in the Father Mathew Hall. *Journey's End* by R. C. Sherriff, the play about life in the trenches during the First World War, was very relevant during the Second. The main reason we decided to do it in fact was because it was suitable for a boys' school. No problems arose, as there were no ladies involved. I think Ria Mooney was the adjudicator on this occasion. She had the narrowest vision about certain things but she was an extremely good teacher. She gave advice strongly and decisively and was, all and all, a very positive figure on these occasions. We won.

The next year, which occurred on or near the centenary of the Famine, we did a fine play by Gerard Healy called *The Black Stranger*. I played Seán the fool, who had a tag line that was almost comic: 'You'll be late for America'. 'The Black Stranger' was a metaphor for the potato blight. Healy died moderately young. I think he was tubercular. He hadn't a big body of work. Adjudicating was J. J. Henry from Dublin. There were lots of groups from Cork and from all over the county. Our rival school in the girls' department, St Al's, had a very strong group. They had a great dramatic tradition because of Eileen Curran, sister of Chris Curran, the actor. She worked very much with another part of the great Cork dramatic tradition, Fr O'Flynn's the Loft. She was a very good actress, both musically and in drama. She played a huge part in the extra work done in St Al's. Maybe the success at the time of St Al's encouraged us as well, just across the river in Pres. One can never forget the interaction between the various groups. I was very well mentioned by Mr J. J. Henry, God be good to him.

We were extremely pleased with our second success, and decided to go for a third year then and picked a completely different play. It was an American play about social pressures and isolationism and being open to the world or locking yourself away. Robert Ardrey's *Thunder Rock* was located on Lake Michigan and was about original settlers coming to America and the taking in of refugees from Europe. This

Dan's certificate for individual acting in Thunder Rock, *1950.*

was of contemporary importance; should one shut oneself off or should one get oneself involved? I played the lighthouse keeper, Charleston.

I presume I saw the Edwards–Mac Liammóir production of it in the Opera House, which would have put it in my mind. The entire thing was very atmospheric. We had an extremely strong cast, having worked together for three or four years. We didn't quite win this time. We drew with St Al's. We would revive the play in 1950 and afterwards for the extension to Pres in 1954.

We won the Independent Cup at the National Festival which was held in the Father Mathew Hall in Dublin, in Church Street. By the time we won the cup in Dublin, we had proved we weren't just a little local group.

You must have learned a lot from the adjudicators.

Yes. *Thunder Rock* was adjudicated by Gabriel Fallon. I remember Der was meticulous in getting things precisely right, so at the entrance to the lighthouse, to convey a proper sense to the audience, Der got

someone to go in a car and get pebbles and stones for the outside of the lighthouse. When Gabriel Fallon came up to do his adjudicating, he was nit-picking. I didn't think he was a great adjudicator but he was a good supporter of the theatre and a good describer of acting. To spoil all our pride and best efforts he remarked, 'I noticed as I came on to adjudicate, an area of stones outside the door. I can't say I noticed the effect that these were supposed to create as a member of the audience. But so much for painstaking realism.' We were chastised.

Later on, I remember Lennox Robinson adjudicating in Killarney. I assume we must have picked the play *Berkeley Square* based on Henry James' short novel, up from the Gate production in the Opera House. Again it was a nice time play where the past and the present were interwoven. I played the lead in it. I must have been putting on a little weight at the time. My leading lady, a girl called Mary O'Carroll, a nice actress, was thin. Lennox didn't care much that we suggested it was a time play. There was a note in the programme saying that the time level in the play shifted backwards and forwards. Lennox said 'It is outrageous that you wrote this note. It has to come across in the performance.' Lennox went on then to say about my leading part as Peter Standish, 'I felt that this actor ought to have been boiled down, and on the contrary his leading lady should have been built up'. As he delivered these words we sat behind him on the stage, not having pleased him too well. The spectacle of Lennox on the stage was an extraordinary one, because steadily throughout he scratched his behind. It didn't matter to the audience obviously. But there we were with a sense of giddiness passing through the company as we looked at the tall, lanky, cadaverous Lennox. That sight, as it were, mitigated the severity of the strictures on our performance.

Lennox Robinson is an interesting writer, isn't he?

He is. He and Daniel Corkery were sometimes referred to as the

Cork Realists. People like Corkery and Lennox Robinson would have been spoken of in a way as making an effort to reflect real Irish life. Lennox Robinson and Corkery had been friends. One of Robinson's plays *The Lesson of His Life* (1909) was staged by the Cork Dramatic Society in An Dún, the small Gaelic League theatre where Corkery's own plays and other original plays were presented.

I think Lennox had some rather astounding qualities. He wrote a fine book called *Three Homes* (1938) about three of the Big Houses that he lived in as a young man around Cork. There was *The Whiteheaded Boy* (1916). I never did it because it was being done all over the place. Then of course there was *Drama at Inish* (1933), where Lennox brought in the idea of the Continental play and the local audience, the hicks dealing with the more adventurous kind of family problems being brought into the world of the parish pump. In *The Big House* (1926), he seemed to catch the genteel world which he would have come from and the wider gombeen world, but delicately worked in and sensitively, in the context of the First World War, the Troubles and the Black and Tans. That was not being done in a lot of the, what you might call peasant, plays of the time. There was an extra note, an extra range, a kind of a Chekhovian quality in it. *The Big House* was successfully revived in the Abbey this summer [2007]. I saw it in one of the festivals years ago and thought it showed sensitive writing on complex themes of identity and belonging. I saw at least one other lovely play, *Killycreggs in Twilight* (1937), in which he really caught a subtle mood.

Tell me about The Ringer, *another of your schoolboy productions.*

Let's just say that we weren't of course taken up with the idea of doing fancy plays only for drama festivals. We also had fun. If you look at the list of productions by PTG you'll find a good deal of farces and comedies and things done for basic enjoyment. My own

Dan in The Ringer *1944.*

longest memory is of having, for a young man, a fairly strong, heavy voice. I always seemed to be doing the 'heavies', however inappropriate I looked. There was quite an idiotic photograph of me playing Dr Lomond in Edgar Wallace's *The Ringer* that we did in the Father Mathew Hall, shortly after our first production of *Journey's End*. I remember it being a glorious uninhibited bit of fun. There had been a Clopet–Yorke production of it in the Opera House in 1939.

We were beginning to find our way. In the school, I remember Brother Evangelist, the principal, a very nice, charming Kerry man, but old-fashioned. There was at least one part in *The Ringer* done by a person who was quite a good comic actor, Dan Fenton. I think he played one of these transvestite roles, one of these kind of Dame parts. We approached Brother Evangelist and we said we wanted to extend the range of the Drama group. And the first question was 'Now will there be girls in it?' We said 'Yes', and oddly enough, he didn't bat an eyelid. Brother Vincent, assistant to Brother Evangelist, kept a rather close eye on what was going on at that time. In fact our female actors became a vital and extremely talented part of our efforts.

Did Presentation Theatre Guild not confine its membership to pupils at the college?

We in PTG were part of the past pupils' union. The advantage of that was enormous. We had the run of the college, rehearsal space, all kinds of general facilities and backing. The result was that PTG became gradually over a couple of years a normal, fully developed drama society and recruited some splendid people who remained loyal to us for years. We did not totally restrict ourselves to Pres people.

Because of doing my Matric in fifth year I must say I had a wonderfully relaxed Leaving Cert year. I had no worries about university exams. Brother Austin had founded the Debating Society around 1938 or '39 and had played a very active part in school life. When I came back to teach in Pres in 1947, I became chairman of it. The tradition carries on. This kind of activity linked to my theatre interests; it was quite a complementary activity. The extra bit of leisure in sixth year allowed me to pursue many such interests, most of them theatrical.

When I finished my Leaving Cert I was approached by Brother Evangelist, who ran the whole school from a notebook and a press. In his gentle Kerry accent he said 'Wouldn't you think of doing the University Scholarship exam? You didn't miss the Inter Scholarship by too much and with your literary subjects' – I was hopeless at maths, I was the bane of Freddie Holland's life but did manage to pass honours maths – 'you might easily gain a Honan or County Council scholarship.' It had been the last thing on my mind because I had such a pleasant Leaving Cert year and felt that I was finished with study for the moment. It was a university-set exam which involved a wider range of work in certain subjects. It was loosely based on the Leaving Cert but with particular emphasis on the essays. There was a mass of reading to be done. The exam was a few weeks after the Leaving. Through that excellent, relaxed Leaving Cert year I had probably recovered somewhat from the trauma and the strain of my father's and my mother's deaths. The challenge got to me. Brother Vincent encouraged me. He was known as 'the Vinc'. Like Brother Evangelist, he taught Latin and was later principal. I did a month of the hardest study in my life. As a reward I earned a County Council scholarship to UCC. It made an enormous difference to my life there.

2

UCC and Daniel Corkery

Was the scholarship to UCC enough?

I was supported here at home in Turner's Cross by my aunt Kit who was teaching at South Presentation Convent and by Patty in Dunmanway. It's not of very great relevance but there was another young boy in our family called Martin. He died in infancy. I was then the youngest and I was to some degree spoiled and cosseted with all these women around me, sisters and aunts. I was carefully nurtured. We were a very well-spaced family. Maybe my parents planned that or maybe other babies died. As I was fourteen when my mother died and nine when my father died I never did find out. I was born at home on 29 May 1926. Mrs Essie O'Regan, midwife of the parish and a great friend of my mother's, delivered me. My mother thought very highly both of her skills and her warmth. Patty was about fifteen when I was born. She was always very caring. My earliest memory is of being wheeled around in the pram by Patty, with what degree of security I don't know, as she talked to her friends in the neighbourhood. Patty's care intensified after my mother died in 1941.

I had the scholarship so that paid my fees. Also because Arts fees weren't very large, I had sufficient to buy a fair number of books. I wasn't too badly off. There was always 'a good table'. I was well nourished and led a reasonably comfortable life. Betty, third in the family, lived here as well. Betty was like Kit, artistic, sensitive and a bit withdrawn. She was very pretty with blonde hair and blue eyes. I'd talk everything out with Betty, who was five years older than me. When my aunt Kit died in the 1970s, Betty asked me not to break up the house. She'd seen the endless sequence of dreary flats that Kit moved to and from at various intervals, before coming here to Turner's Cross. Betty would have liked to be a doctor but the finances wouldn't allow that. Her annoyance with Tim was that in going so slowly with his medical studies, he blocked that.

Tim was in the house here still when I started College. My mother had adored Tim but I was a bit critical of him because of the time he took to do medicine and the worry that was to my mother. I had to modify that criticism of Tim. He was a bad asthmatic and one of the worst experiences of my life was when we were just into the house in Cork, I was still about fourteen or fifteen and Tim had a violent attack of asthma. He was incapable of giving himself the adrenaline injection, so yours truly had to do it. Tim instructed me in finding the vein. That was the situation. We husbanded our resources and we survived.

It was nonetheless a very difficult time. We were still disturbed by the deaths of my father and mother. I signed on in October 1944. Very luckily I had got the scholarship, thanks to the proddings of my teachers. It was very necessary for me to make my own way without delay. The challenge was to become independent, and earn my own living as quickly as possible. There was of course a natural tendency for me, because of the teaching tradition in my mother's family, to do an Arts degree. That would give me a double option. It would enable me to take up teaching and secondly, by choosing maybe the right subjects, I could take up theatrical work. I was already by that time, after my latter years in school and the three-in-a-row at the Drama Festival, very heavily involved in theatre.

We started in UCC[6] as young people do. A good group came together and we re-started the Dramatic Society. I was smitten with the idea of some sort of a stage career, but on what basis I couldn't tell you at the time, because of the War and the conditions around, the uncertainty, the poverty and the sense of isolation.

How isolated did you find Cork during the War?

I think we felt it was very isolated; the University itself was a very small place, with about eight or nine hundred students. There was a very idiosyncratic bunch of professors and lecturers but also it had an extraordinary unity and friendliness.[7] Because of its compact, warm nature you knew everybody. You got to know the staff and the people of the different faculties. It was a very, very pleasant place. I must say I enjoyed my university career enormously and I was stuck in everything. But I think we did feel we were rather cut off. It was very inward-looking. It used its own people, whereas now you have selection committees that appoint the most highly qualified applicants. Much of it, as far as I could see, was rigged to keep good local people working there. While it might be unfair, it did mean you had a very compact, warm and intimate atmosphere, with good contact between staff and students.

Were there many events like plays, concerts, guest lectures; things like that?

During the War we were a little bit confined, because people couldn't travel easily. There were limitations. A man who had a tremendous influence on me, with whom I worked all my life until he died in 1992, was the youngest professor in UCC at the time, Aloys Fleischmann.[8] His people had come to Cork in the late nineteenth century. His father was organist in the North Cathedral and conducted the choir. His mother, Tilly, was a well-known concert pianist. So they had

Joan Denise Moriarty.

already by the 1930s brought in a tremendous Continental influence. Fleischmann[9] as a young man of 26 set out to establish a strong musical department in College. He was very conscious of the need to spread all this extra musical knowledge to the city in general. Cork owes a huge debt to this talented family.

The first thing was he got people around him, and founded the Cork Symphony Orchestra and the Cork Orchestral Society in the 1930s, and organised regular concerts in the City Hall. He also then worked, and brought me in quite early on as a kind of willing body, with the Art Society in the University. That meant we had recitals. Charles Lynch gave a recital very often. I suppose he could do with a little bit of cash at the time. You had other people then, through the years, for example singer Sophie Wyss and Kathleen Long, a very good pianist. You had various local activities beginning to develop, for example the beginning of the Ballet Company with Joan Denise Moriarty.

I remember Joan Denise Moriarty[10] coming on the scene. She was starting to teach dance. I think she originally came from Mallow. But she started classes and I remember her performing with the bagpipes, Fleischmann's splendid arrangement of *Clare's Dragoons,* Thomas Davis's poem, in 1945. I remember seeing her at rehearsals swinging down the Aula Max in UCC with her vivid red hair and striking movement. She made a powerful visual effect. That work was done subsequently in the City Hall. Fleischmann was certainly beginning to get things moving in a big way.

We were all involved when the Blech Quartet recital lost a bit of money. Fleischmann had already exhausted his credit with willing members of staff. He sent me around to try to get a few quid to cover the fees of the unfortunate Quartet, who weren't getting very much anyway. I remember Dr Kelly in

Aloys Fleischmann.

the Physics Department saying to me, 'Dan, tell Fleischmann to do his own dirty work.' I think they were all quite supportive of what he was doing. He handed me a fiver for the good cause.

Tell me about Daniel Corkery in UCC.

Professor Stockley had been there. Patty had studied under him. There was a famous row for the position of Professor of English when Professor Stockley retired around 1931. At any rate there were three or four candidates. Of course O'Faolain was the more highly qualified of the two main candidates, O'Faolain and Corkery. The professorship was an arduous job. There was no particular specialised back-up. Corkery was strongly backed by the Vocational Education people, with whom he had been working very hard.

Daniel Corkery.

Sean O'Faolain in Rome, 1974. (RTÉ)

I think Alfie O'Rahilly as president played a rather dubious role in the appointment. Possibly Alfie was at first impressed more by O'Faolain's[11] academic credentials. O'Faolain had of course left Cork. He had lectured in America. He had his university degree, and had the scholarship throughout College. He had done all sorts of extra-curricular work. And he would have been obviously the most experienced and qualified person to succeed Stockley. Stockley wanted Corkery, maybe again for national reasons. But O'Faolain's nationalist background was of the highest degree. He had served his intellectual apprenticeship with Corkery – like Séamus Murphy, Seán Hendrick and Frank O'Connor, all three of whom had been taught by him in national school.

I think Alfie realised he couldn't bring off the O'Faolain appointment and furthermore he probably did not want to be too associated with one or the other of the candidates. And the result was when UCC were making the appointment, Corkery was chosen above O'Faolain and O'Faolain naturally was furious. Corkery was a safer pair of hands for Alfie. He might be less assertive than O'Faolain. Alfie with his authoritarian views might be bringing in an enemy onto his own pitch if O'Faolain got the job. I have in my possession some old Art Society correspondence with Alfie blocking an invitation to O'Faolain to lecture at the Art Society. I met O'Faolain a few times when he was on a committee for radio in Cork with Máire Ní Mhurchú, Mary Leland and a few others. I found him extremely nice and I think he felt that Alfie shafted him.

Corkery's advantages were that he was known to be an excellent and inspiring teacher. I think O'Faolain did remark in later years that had he got the job, he would have had to give it up within a few years. He would have been frustrated by the limitations of it. But it was a further embitterment of the kind of break that had already occurred between O'Faolain and Corkery and also Frank O'Connor and Corkery. Frank O'Connor was never quite as hostile to Corkery as O'Faolain would have been for a while. I think O'Connor remembered him always with some degree of affection and never denied the kind of influence he had over him as an inspirer and teacher in his younger days.

What would you say about Alfie O'Rahilly, president of UCC then?

Alfie had an extraordinary influence on the development of UCC during those years. I must admit I had very mixed feelings about dealing with him, as I think did a lot of students at the time. He was brusque, a little bit ill mannered, I found. It really was quite frightening to go into his office to get him to agree to something or another. Most things had to meet with his say-so. There was no way of starting out on your own, even with plays. There was, I suppose, what you could only call a censorship that prevailed. There was someone in authority, church or university or state, who kept an eye on what you did. So Alfie was certainly very careful. He was also very conscious about the autonomy of the University, of the fact that you looked after your own; in a sense looking after Corkery, for example, whose MA was given for *Synge and Anglo-Irish literature* (1931). Corkery was a trained national teacher. His MA degree was honorary, a bitter fact for O'Faolain who had better qualifications.

When I was secretary of the Philosophic Society as the Debating Society was called, we were invited to a joint debate of some kind in Trinity in Dublin. We passed on the invitation that had just come through. We were looking to see if we could go and of course get a grant to go. It involved what might be a nice, interesting weekend in Trinity. I'd never been there. I went to Alfie to get his permission and maybe a few bob. I was greeted with a tirade about going to Trinity and 'these people' and we have nothing to do with them and we don't like what they stand for. I was reeling at being assaulted with this level of hostility. His secretary, whom I found extremely kind, ushered me aside and said 'Carry on now, I'll look after this for you'. She acted very kindly because she asked me to come back a few days later. She had got around Alfie and Alfie said to us 'Ye can go, ye can go and if ye like, ye can stay up there altogether.' So we had a very graceless acceptance of our visit to Trinity.

My second encounter was censorship. It really brought it home to me. I had heard of a very good play, very dark, very serious by François Mauriac, the great French novelist. It would translate as *The Stranger*. An English tutor comes into a very high-class French family and the tension is set up between the family and the stranger, the different cultural entity coming in from outside. I thought this would be a good play to do. You had the outsider and you had romantic entanglements and so on. The script was difficult to get. But when it arrived Alfie just blasted me out of it: 'We don't want that kind of Catholicism here.' So again I reeled. I got a lecture on our traditions and their traditions and that sort of thing – the theology of sin, the dark underside of man. Alfie preached the Irish thing to the ultimate degree, the traditional line and under no circumstances would the drama group in UCC do a play by François Mauriac. Even though Alfie hadn't read the play. This one I didn't win.

Even the annual College rag for civic charity was carefully monitored. The students would have to line up in their costumes with their banners and slogans and present themselves for inspection lest anything indecent would pass onto the sober and moral streets of Cork. Alfie and Canon Bastible, Dean of Residence, a singularly pompous man if I may say so, would always check or ensure that groups were checked by their agents. On one occasion in my time in UCC they found a rather safe-looking student bearing a banner for Phil the Fluter's Ball. No notice was taken. But there was a sudden shock when at the end of the back row of the gathered rag community, one of Alfie's agents spotted a banner with 'Phil the Fluter's Other Ball'! Immediate action was taken ...

Didn't Alfie O'Rahilly end up in the religious life?

He did. When he retired he went for the priesthood. He had been married of course. He had two children. He was widowed, and when he retired from the University in 1950 he decided to go for the Church and was ordained as a priest. He trained with the Holy Ghost Fathers to learn to do whatever was felt was required to prepare him for the priesthood.

He would have lived in the Quad in UCC at the time of his presidency?

He would have. The president's residence began to change then. He was probably the last president to use it as living quarters; most of them afterwards preferred their own houses. I think he was in some ways, in the censorship sense, a malignant, rather domineering force although I think administratively he did a lot for the University. But he wouldn't exactly be an endearing figure.

Despite the severity of some of my feelings about Alfie I have to record that I was in grateful receipt of the O'Rahilly medal in 1944–5, for wider-ranging participation in student activities, including the Philosophic Society.

How many people were in the English class when you went to UCC in 1944?

In the main pass classes you might have up to 70 or 80. The honours class might have 25–30. Corkery lectured on the upstairs first floor in the west wing in the Quad. He operated in one of the middle rooms there. With only one assistant he had to run the whole Department on his own. As a matter of fact he took a course in Old English to try to cover that area. In UCC he had to deal with everything from

Conferring of MA degree in English 1952. Front row l–r: UCC President O'Rahilly (centre) with two clergymen. Back row l–r: Ned Gleeson, Ralph Sutton, Dan Donovan.

Shakespeare, to the Metaphysicals, to Pope, the Romantic writers and the Moderns. There was no room for specialisation or no finance to provide some kind of expert cover among the various branches of literature.

While studying English in my earlier years there Bob Breathnach, and later B. G. MacCarthy, taught Old English. Corkery had to do all the rest of it, Shakespeare for instance, and the whole gamut of English literature, even people that would not have been very congenial for him like Pope. To call it a 'Department' was pushing it. There were only two of them later and they had to do it all too. Bob and B. G. MacCarthy had to correct essays as well as everything else. You had to contribute a few essays a term so there was really a very heavy workload. The money wasn't very great. Corkery was on £600 a year or thereabout in the early part of his professorship. Bob started the tutorial system, and I spent ten or eleven years as a tutor in the English Department. We would each have a group of nine or ten whose essays we would correct and record. We would meet once a week in tutorial classes to do whatever really the students wanted us to do. But that was a later development.

What about B. G. MacCarthy, the professor after Corkery?

B. G. would have been coming on at the time. She had written a pioneering study[12] on women writers of the eighteenth century and was play-writing. She was moved in as assistant to Corkery so that she would succeed him.

Corkery retired at the end of my primary degree in 1947, so I had his last three years of teaching. Corkery's assistant Bob, whom I knew very well, was also greatly influenced by Corkery. Bob was temporarily exiled to the Irish Department only to return as lecturer in Old and Middle English and in turn to succeed B. G. MacCarthy as professor. The convolutions of Alfie's manipulations come out here.

Who were your buddies in UCC?

Tomás Ó Laidhin, son of Professor Lyons of the Dairy Science Department, is a lifelong College friend of mine. He won a Travelling Studentship to Oxford. He was a historian and afterwards went into the civil service. John A. Murphy, later Professor John A., was there right through my years in College. We were there doing our ordinary BA together. The most important one in terms of drama was Seán Ó Tuama. I acted like 'a midwife' to two important dramatists, Seán Ó Tuama in the Irish drama and John B. Keane at a later stage. Seán Ó Tuama wrote a body of about eight plays up to the late 1960s. I was involved in almost every one of them, both with production and performance. I collaborated closely with him. Seán merited a Travelling Studentship also which gave him a crucial post-war Continental experience. Seán was influenced by what he saw and got the idea maybe that he might be able to write plays. We at home could read about this changing world. Seán experienced it first-hand and brought it home to us. He was a real inspiration.

He spent a lot of time in Paris in the mid 1950s and came in touch there with the new French drama, which was very interesting due to the existentialist philosophy and the attempt of French writers to see their way through the opaque misery of the Occupation and the divisions that it left. One remembers Beckett in rural France and Paris afterwards. Seán was aware as well of the sort of revolution that Brecht had been making. He saw the opportunity of alerting himself to the new possibilities, the new drama, a getting away from the old-fashioned, well made play to plays with shorter scenes, use of music and expressionism, even the Theatre of the Absurd.

Seán had a very powerful sense of the native culture and language that he picked up from his family and from Corkery, who taught him in UCC. In a sense Corkery had become rather an isolated figure and Seán maybe quite consciously and very deliberately extended the basic philosophy of Corkery to the post-war modern world. He took steps towards applying Corkery's powerful but narrow philosophy rooted in traditional values to a changed and changing world. Of course Seán had splendid Irish. He felt at home writing only in Irish.

Seán said that Corkery's influence was so powerful that it took him years to get out from under his shadow. In a special tribute to Corkery presented by Compántas Chorcaí in the School of Music, Seán selected a little anthology of the essence of Corkery, including excerpts from the seminal works. I had a big part in the presentation, reading in full Corkery's early elemental story 'The Ploughing of Leaca na Naomh' (1916). This is an extraordinary, powerful, primitive story, which in many ways represents the finest example of Corkery's style. Donall Farmer was involved in that 1958 tribute. We also presented Corkery's political play about the 1916 Rising, which was written in Irish.

His Hidden Ireland *(1924) is sometimes viewed as the first post-colonial text.*[13]

Corkery's *The Hidden Ireland* (1924) expounded a different approach to the history, if you could call it a history, of Irish literature. The title explains this: *The Hidden Ireland;* the poets that are not backed by any institution or government, who are not backed by any state, the hedge poets you might call them, who worked in the most bleak and troublesome conditions. Those poets, the Maigue Poets, Ó Súilleabháin, and Aogán Ó Rathaille for example were adjuncts of some of the old Gaelic families. All that is the hidden side, that was brought out in *The Hidden Ireland.* Corkery was anxious that all that had to come into the light of day and take its part beside the very well written literary history of the more recent Anglo-Irish movement.

Why did Corkery become isolated?

I think he became very rigid and old and disappointed with the way things developed. In his early years, the years of *The Hidden Ireland* and the early volumes of short stories and of course the fine poetic novel of frustrated Cork life, *The Threshold of Quiet* (1917), Corkery was a very great creative artist. He was also a great theorist and teacher. As a lifelong member of the Gaelic League, I think he became trapped in a little isolated world that began to be increasingly alienated from change and modern developments. I think his basic teachings were profound and deep rooted but he had become a bit of an anachronism and inward-looking in some ways. I suppose you could prove it by the fact that certainly O'Connor and O'Faolain would have been very deeply influenced by him, his teaching and his nationalism during the struggle for freedom. Their more flexible nationalism in turn caused them to fall out with him. In the summer of 1926, the year I was born, in the *Irish Tribune* O'Connor, O'Faolain, Seán Hendrick and Corkery debated issues of tradition and nationhood quite hotly.[14]

O'Faolain and O'Connor later became 'the bright young men'. 'Bright' was a very important word to Corkery. 'Bright' young men, men like Frank O'Connor and O'Faolain wrote for American magazines like *The New Yorker*, breaking Corkery's strong conviction of writing only for an Irish suffrage. He did not particularly approve of people he called 'bright'. He felt they were rather superficial, flashy; flashiness of any kind was a rather dirty word, in a sense of being too brilliant in a kind of surface and personal, subjective way. And he was bitterly disappointed in his two great pupils, who in a broader and better sense were really 'bright' and greatly extended the boundaries of Irish writing. The last time he met O'Connor, on the street in Cork in 1956, Corkery said 'Well, if it isn't Mr O'Connor, who only writes for American magazines now' and passed on.[15] I think that was the last word for one of his great pupils, the most deeply influenced by him in many ways.

And of course they were all deeply involved in the nationalist movement. They were active members of the IRA. Corkery himself wasn't a militarist. But Frank O'Connor and O'Faolain were caught up in the movement, thanks to Corkery's nationalism. O'Connor was interned up in the Women's Gaol I think, and in Gormanstown near Dublin in 1923.

In my mother's library in the house in Ballincollig, her books would have brought me to Corkery. *The Hidden Ireland* was in the house, as it was in most educated houses. It was a flawed but a most seminal book. It touched chords that were very stimulating and people found the whole culture of Ireland was broadened to include *The Hidden Ireland*. Writers totally neglected by established critics had led almost secret lives due to the language problem. *The Hidden Ireland* with all its flaws and historical inaccuracies changed the way we looked at Irish history and culture for the twentieth century.

The Threshold of Quiet is perhaps the best Cork novel but he chose to see it as a dead end which he decided not to pursue. In his subsequent writing career, his main creative efforts were devoted to the short story which greatly influenced his pupils, even if, as often, they reacted against his example. I liked *A Munster Twilight* (1916) and *The Hounds of Banba* (1920). One of the last books of short stories was *The Stormy Hills* (1929). I remember getting that as a school prize in Pres. He had taught with the Pres Brothers in the old South Monastery in Douglas Street and remembered them. He used to ask me about them. 'Tell me,' he used to say, 'how is Berchmans Boyce?' (the principal in Pres when I entered the secondary school in 1939). I fancied he liked the alliteration but there was genuine affection.

Corkery would have been a familiar presence to me on a social level. I would have seen him fairly regularly because when he became professor he went to live in Ballygroman near Ovens. I used to see him with his sister Mary attending eleven o'clock Mass, second Mass in Ballincollig church, Ballygroman being only three miles or so west of Ballincollig. After he retired, he bought his little bungalow overlooking Poll Gorm in Myrtleville. He loved the little house and on one visit there I remember him talking about the extraordinary way the red flashing light of the old Daunt rock lightship illuminated and warmed the great stretch of sea that lay between his house and it. It was a rather lonely place in winter for himself and his sister Mary. Seán Hendrick, Bob Breathnach and other friends and colleagues visited him there. I frequently visited him or met him on the coast road to Fountainstown. He would have his little easel and sketching materials as he continued his lifelong devotion to painting. I was in Dublin at his exhibition in Waddington's a couple of years before Waddington went to London [in 1957]. Tom Lyons and I went. After Corkery's death Charlo Quain gathered together some of the paintings and put on an exhibition in Lavitt's Quay.

What did Corkery look like?

Small, very lame of course, which limited his physical scope, red cheeked, white haired with a weak rather hoarse voice. Some complained of the narrowness of range of his writing but this was inevitably thrust upon him because of his lameness and background and belief that it was only in the Irish language that Ireland could express itself to itself. He came to feel that even his own creative efforts were futile, because they were in English. He walked with a very pronounced limp. He was almost cut off from a good deal of the ordinary experience of a young man of his time and he had a slightly more introverted view because of his circumstances, which did enable him to write *The Threshold of Quiet*. But he produced little of major importance after 1931, when he gathered many earlier essays and lectures into the superb *Synge and Anglo-Irish literature*, to acquire the MA and earn the chair of English. The superb teaching remained.

I think there was an internal conflict in Corkery between his appreciation of powerful, personal Romantic feeling and the stricter, more Classical criteria that he would have developed in his theories about literature. They didn't sit easily together. This might in some ways have silenced him. For him the personal subjective way was not the way to go. He was very aware of Eliot's 'objective correlative', a way of expressing emotion through a system of imagery avoiding direct subjectivity. This would lead to an austere and disciplined way of dealing with emotion, added to by the circumscribed nature of his life. But maybe he was losing touch with the more practical world.

Shortly after he retired, himself and Lord Mayor Cronin went around the main streets in the centre of the city in a Landau carriage, renaming the streets, giving them Irish names in place of the old British ones that had graced our streets for so long. It struck me as a quixotic gesture. It had, as far as I know, no legal binding. If the streets of Cork were baptised into the Gaelic world on a Saturday they would have to be unbaptised rather rapidly on Monday morning when all the tenants and professionals dealt with their post.

Patrick Maume, a former Pres student, has a very good assessment of Corkery in his book.[16]

3

An Older World of Cork Theatre

When I read about this period in that book edited by Ruth Fleischmann,[17] to which you contributed, it strikes me as a period of great optimism and co-operation.

Yes, that was a marvellous thing. We spoke earlier about the sense of isolation during the War. All of a sudden things started to happen. There was an opening out, and there was activity. The city was coming to life and indeed during the 1950s that simply grew and grew. For instance from College and from helping with the Fleischmann recitals and even getting my first broadcast, my first few words on the air occurred. I already did a fair bit of dramatic work and if I say so myself spoke verse fairly well.

Your love for verse and for complex text was always there.

Yes. With Lesley Horne, our College drama group, the Ballet Company and the Orchestral Society, there were a number of productions that were very interesting. The first of them I remember was Milton's *Comus* (1634), presented in the Father Mathew Hall in 1947 or 1948. There was a huge cast, splendid scenery, dancing and music. I had the lead part of Comus. I liked Milton's poetry. I studied it in university – parts of *Paradise Lost* and *Samson Agonistes*. At any rate *Comus* is quite a nice lyrical text. As a villain, the part of Comus gave me a fair bit of scope.

It was difficult speaking because there was a good deal of rhyming couplets as well.

Alec Day did the scenery. There was a trinity of people who were all putting their oar into the work of production, which sometimes irritated us. 'The Big Three' discussed or argued while the combined company waited onstage. I worked with people like Lorna Daly, Eileen Brennan and Sylvia O'Shaughnessy, all performers who were of importance. Ballet wasn't my forte and I had moves to fit in with the corps de ballet. I had to get to Joan Denise on a descent at one point and my worry was that my timing was a little off and she could come down too heavily. And she did one night. I was afraid I would do permanent damage to her internally but she survived. I was no great dancer, on or off the stage.

Lesley Horne did the casting, as I remember. He arranged the script of the masque. As I remember the general production overall was done by Donald Beavan, an impressive singer and a good actor. With a certain amount of exasperation he kept the show on the road, especially during rehearsals with the whole lot of dancers, singers, actors and musicians. These elaborate productions were all beautifully mounted and would certainly have inspired me for the future. I was involved in three more: Purcell's *The Fairy Queen* twice and Ibsen's *Peer Gynt* with Grieg's music.

What was Alec Day, from a very prominent merchant family among whom there were excellent photographers,[18] *like?*

He was a rather large man, a large tweedy man and very interested in the visual side of things. I found him pleasant but a little remote.

Tell me what was Day's shop on 103 Patrick Street like?

It had tackle, fishing and leather goods; that kind of thing if my memory serves me rightly. It was an old and very well regarded business. Good quality, nicely displayed quality stock.

That production of Comus *was different to a regular stage play.*

Yes, it was an effort really to bring a bit of imagination to the stage in Cork. I think as well because so much of this was going on, the idea of bringing verse back into plays affected Seán Ó Tuama, especially in his earlier plays. The influence of T. S. Eliot and Yeats would have turned our minds in that direction. There was a hope that verse plays might come back as a common medium of expression within plays but it was a false dawn. But there was a string of verse plays by some of the most distinguished poets writing in English at the time, most notably Eliot. Louis MacNeice's verse plays I became familiar with by listening to the BBC Third Programme, a huge cultural lift to anyone interested in the arts. His translation of Goethe's *Faust,* his play about Christopher Columbus and *The Dark Tower* were written for broadcasting. Even though he lived in Kinsale for a time before his death in 1963, I never met him. I did hear about him. His wife had a restaurant there.

We haven't talked about the role the Opera House played in your apprenticeship.

John Daly thoroughly used the visiting companies. I can recall Lord Longford coming up to Pres with Lady Longford, when Longford Productions were in the Opera House, to speak about the theatre to the students. All the Dublin seasons were replicated later in the Opera House. When I look at the list of Pres plays I see that we did two plays that the Gate did, *Berkeley Square* and *Thunder Rock,* the last in our three-in-a-row Cork Drama Festival successes.

When PTG won the Drama Festival, it gave us our artistic base.[19] John Daly immediately invited *Journey's End,* as winning play of the Cork Father Mathew Festival, to perform for a week in the Opera House. He was a very humorous man and had a gift for teaching. When we were transferring from the Father Mathew Hall, John did a great deal of work with us. I remember he came up to our rehearsals in Pres. John re-jigged the productions to being suitable and proportionate to the much bigger space at the Opera House. In *Journey's End*, Sherriff's First World War play, the collapse of the dug-out was extremely lively and often you heard 'the holy name' from the audience as the bang went off.

When we won with *The Black Stranger*, we had another week in the Opera House and subsequently had a further production. We did a farce, *Tons of Money*, in 1945. From the middle to late 1940s I was beginning to get quite active in the Opera House. As well as that I did a few productions with the Little Theatre Society [LTS] in its later slightly more enfeebled days. Through these circumstances I got well in with the Opera House and got to know all the people working there.

The old Cork Opera House.

The Opera House was very beautiful, very dilapidated, and atmospheric with the smell of paint and the smell of cats on the stage. It was a lovely space, bigger than the Everyman Palace, with a good-sized stage with lovely acoustics. If, for example, you had amplification in it like in a modern theatre you would blast people out of it completely. It was a lovely intimate space, horseshoe shaped with no soft seating in the gods. There was bench seating. There was an external climb up to the gods. You can see the old photos of it. You had a lovely dress circle. And you had a great old staff who were there for years.

Passion plays were usual during Lent at the time and we did several, including *The Trial of Christ* which in 1952 was specially translated for us by Dr Staf Gebruers, *carillonneur* at Cobh Cathedral, from a Flemish original. We nicknamed this play *The Ear* because of the big emphasis in the plot on the cutting off of the High Priest's servant's ear, by Peter. We were regulars at the Opera House by this time.

Where would you normally get your scripts?

The great blessing was French's Acting Edition. French's did huge work for the amateur movement. They had a big list, and you would order them from London. They also collected the fees and performance royalties on behalf of the authors. You would write directly to London and they would quote the royalty fees for the performance of any plays they controlled or managed. It was a very good operation. All the movements of the play and the stage directions were printed with the dialogue. A handy short cut for the lazy or amateur director.

Even though Frank O'Connor left Cork when you were a babe in arms, his role in Cork theatre is legendary.

It was Frank O'Connor who always had the feeling no town or city was worth a damn if it didn't have some sort of drama going on. It was one of the tests. He would have known about Corkery's

French's Licence to Der Breen, 1945.

Dún in what was in effect the west end of Cork, old Queen Street, now Father Mathew Street. Coincidentally, the Dún was near the Father Mathew Hall. It was an effort, on the basis of what had been done at the Abbey, to create a basis for Cork theatre, of Cork provenance. That gradually died away by 1913, when O'Connor himself was still a child. The basis on which Corkery established the Dún would have been a little bit too narrow. It would have to widen out, regardless of content, regardless of how technique was concerned. Theatre was always changing, altering. The emphasis was always on altering the way things were presented so you wouldn't restrict yourself imaginatively and get tied down. Geraldine and Seán Neeson

Frank O'Connor.

and some others saw the Dún as a bit too narrow. O'Connor, the Neesons, Mac Liammóir and Seán Hendrick started the Cork Drama League in 1927.[20] Nancy McCarthy and the Neesons and a whole lot of other people were active in the literary movement and would have been in the Dún. Seán [Neeson] wasn't a great actor, but he did cameo parts. Geraldine was a superb character actress.

The debut play for the Cork Drama League in Gregg Hall on South Mall was Lennox Robinson's *The Round Table*. Their second production was a Chekhov, *The Cherry Orchard*. Nancy was also in that. She was doing a line with Frank at the time. She got the lead and even though she had a stutter, she got through. They stayed very friendly. She always talked about her Michael: Michael O'Donovan was his name. It was time for O'Connor to leave Cork and when he went to Dublin late in 1928 the impetus went out of the Cork Drama League.

Nancy might have been older than Betty but due to their common involvement in pharmacy they knew one another. Because of their mutual interest in the arts, they became friendly. They became, in time, mature spinster ladies of that ilk. Through the Orchestral Society and through Betty, I came to know Nancy very well. She was very loyal to the Society and to Aloys Fleischmann. She was a delight.

She took things with a detached humour and very often she had a lovely power of cutting through pretension. Michael O'Donovan's going from Cork would have lessened the bond between her and him. But I have a feeling that Nancy, like Betty, was a born independent woman. Marriage and all that jazz could have contained her with difficulty, due to the range of her interests. I met Frank O'Connor only once. I bumped into him and Nancy on the street. He was a bit distracted. It was a perfunctory meeting.

During the controversy over Cross's *The Tailor and Ansty* (1942) Nancy was fit to be tied at the carry on of the clergy and the burning of Cross's book. She was active in combating all that old-fashioned pietism and the evils done by the censorship authorities, which led to upset and heartbreak for writers trying to make their way. She knew the tailor, Tim Buckley, well and often heard him giving forth in his little house in Gougane Barra. Ballingeary was a Gaeltacht which

Dan Donovan, Chris Curran, Nancy McCarthy, James N. Healy.

they all went to in the summers. She would have known Conny and Dinny 'Gougane' who had hotels there. *The Tailor and Ansty* was full of lovely earthy things. It was Rabelaisian – a highly popular word with Seán Ó Ríordáin. That kind of natural, healthy vulgarity caused the book to be treated so badly. Despite Holy Ireland and the efforts of the thin-blooded puritans in the Gaelic League, Irish *was* a richly Rabelaisian language. The tailor was part of a rich, broadly based culture that called a spade a spade. What Cross was trying to do was give an impression of the tailor that would convey the verbal vigour and richness of the man and his powers of observation. People found him a delight to be with, sensitive and wholly aware of all aspects of life around him.

One of the little stories that caused trouble was the one about the bull, which goes something like this. One day a man called to see a bull. In his usual way the tailor cross-hackled him, as they say, about who he was and where he came from. They were always curious. The man wanted to go and see the fine bull. 'Are you a married man yourself?' the tailor asked. 'I am, I am,' said the man. 'And have you children?' 'I have, I have fifteen'. 'Stand there now' said the tailor 'and I'll bring the bull out to see you.'

You had the same living tradition of Rabelaisian Irish in a different part of Munster with Mike the *File,* Peig Sayers' son. One day, Seán Ó Tuama and Betty his wife and I were down in Graig in Kerry, near where you turn left for Dunquin. We were laughing in wonder at the extent of the vocabulary and the richness of his language. There was an utmost precision in talking about matters such as cow dung. There would be different categories for example for the cow dung on the road, different words to describe it, conveying specific physical conditions. Delargy in the Folklore Commission said that Peig had a virtuoso memory and so had Mike the *File.* So much of that rich language was saved.

And O'Connor himself revelled in it in his post-war translation of Brian Merriman's work. After the Cork Drama League, what theatre group was emerging in the 1930s?

There is a little thread going through, particularly with Geraldine Neeson. Geraldine would have been one of the founders of the next effort to get some sort of a dramatic society that would reflect the city or some aspect of the city, whether literary or life or both. In the early 1930s, the Little Theatre Society was formed. It set out to draw people from some of the dramatic societies and to do plays in a central location, usually the Opera House and to again try and combine two notions that had parted company in the early groups. Geraldine would have been very aware of local plays being done. There were also then a great deal of international plays to be put on, to bridge a gap that had become apparent.

We take in another man who had a part in all this, and had a huge influence on Cork theatre, Fr O'Flynn. There was a murderous row[21] in the *Cork Examiner* around the performing of Shakespeare 'with the dirty words left out' through correspondence between Frank O'Connor and his aims for modern theatre and Fr O'Flynn at the Loft whose main interest, total interest really, was the teaching and perpetuation and development of Shakespeare. Fr O'Flynn was a major actor who was a priest and who wasn't able to perform directly on the stage in those days. I would say he had formidable talents as an actor; power, imagination and vigour but again there was a certain narrowness. He didn't like a lot of the modern world, didn't like modern drama. Whether he knew much about them or not, he didn't have very much time for Ibsen and Chekhov and people like that, whereas people with a broader sense like O'Connor knew where the future lay. There was a very public controversy between the two and O'Connor left Cork shortly after that.

There was a serious split in the Loft. Two of the people who left were Jim Stack and Eddie Golden. The Little Theatre Society was largely founded and directed by Jim Stack, Eddie Golden and Geraldine Neeson. Seán, a lovely man, was strongly active and supportive of the work going on. By the time I came to The Little Theatre Society in the early 1940s, Jim had his own company, Jim Stack Productions.

That then was The Little Theatre Society. They would have drawn in groups like the Good Companions who put on productions in Gregg Hall. Bishop Gregg was the Protestant Bishop involved with the construction of St Fin Barre's Cathedral in the 1860s. Gregg Road near St Fin Barre's Cathedral was named after him. The prominent persons in the Good Companions were Cecil and Bett Marchant.

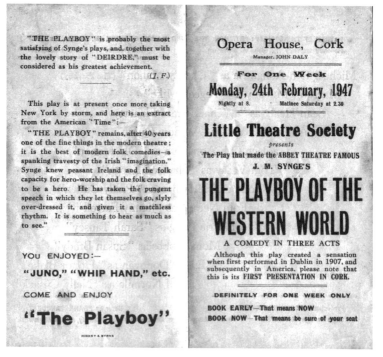

Programme for The Playboy of the Western World, *1947 (cover).*

PATRON OF THE SOCIETY: RT. HON. THE LORD MAYOR OF CORK (M. Sheehan, Esq., T.C.)
Honorary Secretary ... John A. Heffernan ' Hon. Treasurer ... T. O h-Aonghusa

Micheal O h-Aonghusa as " Christy Mahon" (The Playboy)

Margaret Murphy as " Pegeen Mike"

Sean Healy as " Michael James Flaherty"

Aileen de Barra as " Widow Quinn"

Traolach O h-Aonghusa as " Old Mahon"

Tom Vesey as " Shaneen Keogh"

John A. Heffernan as " Philly Cullen"

Eoin Neeson as "Jimmy Farrell"

Norrie Long as " Sarah Tansey"

Mona Hobbs as " Susan Brady"

Eve O'Donovan as " Honor Blake"

Nell Normile as " Nelly Cusack"

Production by CECIL MARCHANT   Decor by FRANK SANQUEST
Stage Manager, Kevin O'Shea   Assistant Stage Manger, Cathal Henry   Publicity, Aveline Marlow

Programme for The Playboy of the Western World, *1947 (inside).*

Cecil was the manager of Piggott & Co., who were the musical and dramatic text people in 117 Patrick Street. There was a very prominent actor in the drama department there, Seán Healy, who worked very actively in the Little Theatre Society. He was a good singer, comedian and character actor. He was a most jovial, lovely man.

How many did the old Opera House seat?

One thousand. There was a lovely mix of plays, apart from the classics. There were the fit-up companies. The legendary Anew McMaster would do quite commonplace things, like *Pink String and Ceiling Wax,* a name that clings to my mind. Some of the McMaster productions were a bit basic. He was a law unto himself. I remember seeing a production of *Trilby* one night and he was playing the piano. It was a record of course and he calmly lit a cigarette as the music merrily played on. Things like that. Mac's seasons of a fortnight in the old Opera House would cover maybe ten plays, largely based on presenting himself in his favourite roles. I saw him about three times in *Othello*. As the years passed Mac seemed to me to get more and more perfunctory in the early Venetian scenes but he never failed to give a tremendous epileptic fit in the second half of the play. It was absolutely stunning. He brought it to a fine art. *Lear* was probably his favourite Shakespeare play, and his Coriolanus was greatly admired at Stratford.

Ian Priestly Mitchell used to do rather pompous, high-sounding, grand-voiced things for the Hospital Sweeps commercials on the radio. His wife was Esmé Biddle, nicknamed 'Red Biddy' by the company. She was occasionally partial to a tipple. She was playing Lady Macbeth one night or maybe Portia and she was a bit the worse for wear. McMaster was muttering at her, 'get up woman, get up woman' in a voice you could hear at the back of the gods. But she was regularly employed; a good actress, a little gone to seed. One morning I met Mac in the theatre when there was a general search going on for Esmé. The standard fear was that she had gone away for a drink. She was found locked in one of the women's dressing rooms. He was quite decent to his actors. I heard of him fishing one of them out of the Blackwater, when they were playing on a stage near the river in Cappoquin. Mac was genuinely concerned for the welfare of his company.

He really presented a wide range of theatre, *Oedipus* for example, and modern plays. Mac's was a great training ground for group players including Harold Pinter. Mac was responsible for bringing Hilton Edwards to Ireland in 1927 and that led of course to the famous partnership of Edwards and Mac Liammóir, which lasted until Mac

Liammóir's death in 1978. McMaster married Mac Liammóir's sister. I met Mary Rose McMaster, Mac's daughter, in Norrie Long's house. It was a great theatre house. They had a kind of a theatrical salon. Norrie Long's brother Bob used to stage-manage the Loft. Bob was very funny. Their sister Ina had a really extraordinary droll wit that often had me and others in stitches at some of the accounts

Anew McMaster.

of back stage carry-on during Fr O'Flynn's marathon seasons of Shakespeare in the old Opera House. They would sometimes do six Shakespeares in a week, which occasionally led to confusion, usually over costumes. The stage manager would often have to say 'In the name of God take those costumes off, it's *Hamlet* tonight laddies!' The actors might have put on the costumes for *The Merchant of Venice*!

I must say Mac was a lousy Macbeth. Both McMaster and Mac Liammóir got into bad habits because they directed themselves. I remember in one of the dark scenes in *Macbeth*, McMaster's stage manager had gone to enormous trouble to give Mac a lighting contraption under his cloak. Mac got the device caught in the cloak and the whole thing had to come out. Mac, always one for the heroic gesture, brandished it before the audience. There was also a specially lit dagger which he completely ignored.

Have you any funny stories about Mac Liammóir and Edwards visiting Cork?

Pork wasn't too common on the menus of restaurants in the 1940s. But the lady who managed the Pavilion restaurant on [80-82] Patrick Street had a very good line in excellent pork. Mac Liammóir and Hilton usually ate in the Pav, and someone sitting next to them one day overheard the order. Mac Liammóir said 'I'll have the pork *dry*.'

We met them all. The Little Theatre Society – at that time in its final years – was run by Geraldine and Seán. They had been in touch with Edwards and Mac Liammóir when they began to set up their Gate Company and the Cork Drama League was beginning.[22] Geraldine and Seán had befriended them in Cork and had smoothed the way for them. We would be brought to a party in the Savoy on Patrick Street, where there was a fine big room. The Gate Company were entertained with all the members of the Little Theatre Society

Micheál Mac Liammóir, Geraldine Neeson with friends, and Hilton Edwards, c. 1960.

and there would be speeches and so on. So that really with the help of all these companies Cork theatre was like a university of theatre. My big crib these days is that the repertory basically doesn't get done. Theatre work is best thought of as an apprenticeship where you learn your trade.

With all this activity and the work of the local operatic societies and the Dublin Grand Opera Society, you had marvellous audiences. You really knew that there was always something worthwhile on at the Opera House. John Daly succeeded in keeping great continuity and managed to keep the House going very well. Support was very good. That continued when John died prematurely in the early 1950s and Bill Twomey the radio broadcaster and rugby commentator took over and maintained the same policy for years.

4

Back to Pres to Teach

You went back to Pres after your BA.

I came back to Pres in 1947 to do my Higher Diploma. I'd got my primary degree in the early autumn. My old school, in fairness to them, made me welcome and I was given the approved number of hours. I was in luck because I found I could also make some money. A Brother got sick – one wishes illness on no one – and I was given his hours and paid for them.

A fine warm overcoat was essential in those days. Not only did we have what I remember as severe winters – a period of frost seemed almost *de rigueur* for winter then – but the ownership of a motor car was a prospect still far in the distance. Central heating in houses wasn't all that plentiful. So the crombie coat I acquired was no status symbol or piece of luxury. It was a necessity in those times.

When I went back to Pres there were only two cars owned by staff. Paddy Geraghty had had a heart attack so he had a small Morris and Kevin Harty had a baby Ford. Having a Ford was a matter of civic loyalty. I eventually gained my first second-hand Ford Anglia via a Triumph motorbike and a scooter. Any time there was a half day in Pres, friendly teachers would head off to the seaside, weather permitting. The usual suspects were Paddy Geraghty, a Dublin man who had taught in Pearse's school, Scoil Éanna, Danny Duggan, a great Latin teacher who lived on Western Road, and sometimes John Dorgan from Blackpool. I think when John Dorgan stopped his travels with us, Declan Healy joined in. Declan is the nephew of Gus Healy, the stalwart on the VEC for many years, and the first lay principal in Pres. Alfie Madden, of the Holland and Madden maths book, used come along and Bill Driscoll, our Science teacher from Drimoleague. We would have a swim if the weather was good. We would preferably go to a place which had a good hotel or restaurant. The day would culminate in a good old-fashioned meal. We would talk school, but if circumstances were agreeable we'd have a bit of singing on the way home. When Paddy Geraghty had a couple of half ones inside him, he was always good for *The Minstrel Boy*. Danny Duggan had quite a repertory of songs. There was a sentimental Victorian one about a little drummer boy called Taps, who was injured in battle and died. It brought tears to our eyes. Declan is a very good singer and could give a ballad in Irish. I might contribute a number. I was very partial in those days to songs I knew by Bobby Burns or Stephen Foster. *I Dream of Jeanie*, that sort of thing. We would pass the homeward journey in a very pleasant manner.

At the end of my diploma year I was invited to take a full-time post in Pres. I stayed for the rest of my life. My future in that sense was settled. Coming back to Pres was like coming home or coming to another home. Brothers changed very regularly, maybe every six or seven years. The Order had two schools in Dublin, one in Bray and one in Glasthule. They had schools in Kinsale and Cobh. They had a school in Carrick-on-Shannon and John McGahern in *Memoir* praises Brother Placid who taught him there. There would be a regular rotation of Brothers. But the main lay staff of ten or twelve would vary very little over decades. One hardly noticed them getting older. The place had a peculiarly settled quality. There seemed to be a great psychological stability about the place. It had had the wonderful old

Brother, 'the Man', who imparted his own particular character to the place. Dr Connolly seemed to appear from some corner or other. He was an abiding presence even after he died. He was a small, red-faced man from one of the old butter families in Cork, a fine scholar with an understanding and benevolent nature. The ethos of the school was set by 'the Man' who was there on that site from the beginning [1887].

By contrast there was 'Lolly' who had taught me in Junior School, a tall, upright man with grey hair, another lovely man. 'The Man' never punished anybody. He had a moral authority. I think his strongest form of opprobrium was 'Aren't you a little puppy?' You wouldn't want it applied to you. 'Lolly' had a folded strap in his pocket and if there was any aggression in the yard you'd get it across the legs. Between the two of them they made a great complementary pair. Though rough in his ways 'Lolly', or Loyola, was very kindly. O'Faolain was taught by 'the Man' and has a nice tribute to him in *Vive Moi!*. 'The Man' would have helped him to get a scholarship to UCC in 1918. 'The Man' died during the War. They were both dead when I came back to Pres in 1947.

I got a first class honours Higher Diploma in Education. A nun friend of mine once remarked 'I was delighted to see you left one of our nuns duck in ahead of you'. I got second place in the class. During the Higher Diploma year the drama was looming a bit. I had got a decent primary degree in English and Latin with History as my subsidiary. Jim Hurley, the College Registrar who had graduated with Patty, suggested that the university scholarship might hold if I went on to do a Master's degree. I thought I would like to do the MA. Someone advised me to do it in sequence. Once you broke you might never go back.

I decided to do it by thesis and that involved picking a subject. I decided to increase my possibilities of choice later on, maybe, by picking a theatrical subject. I wanted to get a sense of the wider world into the narrower Gaelic world. I felt that there was a certain narrow Gaelic League world that in some ways bedevilled the development of Irish. I was conscious that there had to be a change in attitudes, there had to be an opening of attitudes. It was beginning to happen anyway. I felt it would be good to pick a subject that marked the practical work of someone who both as a writer and organiser helped the development of theatre in Ireland. I decided to take a middle road and study Lady Gregory and her contributions to the Abbey.[23] Lady Gregory, though not maybe a great writer, was a good writer of considerable range. Her play *Spreading the News* was one of the opening Abbey plays in 1904. She occasionally hit the button. She was very practical; she was in a sense 'the charwoman' of the Abbey. You wrote plays because you needed plays and there weren't enough Irish plays around. She wrote about 40 plays. She would have had some Irish; she'd have gone around and learnt it. She did keep an eye on the international side and did translations of Molière and Goldoni. Lady Gregory as the lady-of-all-work as it were, for many years kept the Abbey going and kept it close to the realities of life, when people like Yeats might be flying off the handle. Yeats's impracticality is sometimes exaggerated. The Abbey survived because of their work.

One of the problems I had was that a lot of the research material including her journals had gone to America after she died in 1932. Luckily, Lennox Robinson had issued a limited selection of them[24] and it was among the books I received for the Peel Memorial Prize in 1947. My professor was of course B. G. MacCarthy. She was extremely kind and extremely helpful. She was in the early years of her professorship and without interfering in any way she was both helpful and systematic. We got on very well together really. I hacked away. She kept warning me to keep my own reactions to the plays coming through.

At any rate I managed to get a first class honours for the thesis. My extern was also very helpful, he had to keep a vague eye on it. He was J. R. R. Tolkien of *The Hobbit* fame. That was the only book of his I had read at the time. That exploration of the practical aspects of theatre maybe laid the seeds of why I never had any urge to write plays. I got caught up in the practical side of theatre, especially when Der Breen left PTG in the mid 1950s. I then became a manufactured director. I had perhaps been a natural actor. As a director you read more and more and in many ways can lose your own voice. I did write a play about school and I found that increasingly I was becoming embarrassed by some material based on my close and not so close friends. It inhibited me. I lacked a certain ruthless quality necessary in a good writer.

You did Noah *with Der Breen just as you were finishing the MA, didn't you?*

Yes, that was in early 1951–1952. André Obey's *Noah* marked the culmination of university drama for me. We were getting ambitious at that stage. We had done a number of light plays. If you remember there was no department of drama at that stage. We were starting from scratch really. We were drawn from everywhere. We did *The Invasion of Carrigroe*; that was a Harry O'Donovan play. We did *House Master* by Ian Hay, a light English farcical comedy. I did a play by Priestley, *Eden End*. We did *The School for Scandal* by Sheridan. Aileen Barry directed. We were very proud of that and I suppose it was giving us ideas. I was facing the fact that I would shortly be leaving the University. I was coming to the end of my MA course. We decided that we would really have a go. We were helped as well by the fact that the staff rep of the drama group was Professor B. G. MacCarthy herself. She said wouldn't it be nice to do something of good high standard as I came to the end of my Dramat career.

B. G. had taken over in Dramat from Professor Sperrin-Johnson. College was full of eccentric professors at the time. I think Sperrin-Johnson was professor of Botany. He was our first encouraging staff representative for Dramat. He lived in Blackrock Castle and we were invited out there regularly. We could rehearse there. He had a magnificent pipe organ down in the basement of Blackrock Castle or on the ground floor. He would occasionally entertain us with Moore's *Love Thee Dearest* before we departed out into the night to catch the Blackrock bus.

Then B. G. took over. It was B. G. who guided us through my last years there. I had possibly read the play *Noah* or maybe heard it. I

Award-winning cast of Noah, *1951. Front row l–r: Der Breen, Jill Busteed, Professor B. G. MacCarthy, Dan Donovan. Middle row l–r: Marie Whelan, Michael McConnell, Patricia Kennedy, Michael Bradley, Denise Scott, Joe O'Sullivan, Sean Lucey. Back row l–r: Gerald Cleary, Cathleen Timmons, Brian McLoughlin, unknown, Winnie O'Leary.*

mentioned earlier that the old Radio Éireann rep made you aware of plays to beat the band. Every Sunday night that splendid company did good productions. I had my ear glued to that great company for so many years. All these plays became a matter of possibility by hearing them and being made aware of them. We got scripts. It seemed really suitable for a 'heavy' like myself. This was probably the 'heaviest' so far but I was getting older. We decided we'd have a go at it for the University Dramatic Association [UDA] festival. That was all the universities coming together. It was held in Galway. Seán Lucey and Pat, his future wife, were there. Seán later became professor of English in UCC. We decided that since I was going to do the main part, we'd get Der Breen to do the production. Der agreed, although he was not a student at UCC. After school Der became a commercial traveller with Joyce's sweet manufacturers. *Noah* was a typical Der production: simple and imaginative. It was a good deal of practical work, which I didn't altogether appreciate at the time – saws and hammers and bits of timber for the ark. The play was about the ark of course, but it was really about the break-up of relationships, typically French, witty and very allusive. It was about other things as well: the nature of time and change, a play of failure of the ambitions and goals that seize people when they are caught up in them and which cause things to fall apart when these goals are achieved or partially achieved. Things fall apart, the centre cannot hold. So it was a rich, lovely play, beautifully written, elegant and at the same time within our means. I loved the part of Noah, we won and I got the cup from the adjudicator, Eleanor Matthews. It was a kind of fizzy climax to my university career and interestingly enough, Seán Ó Tuama was up there with us as well. The origins of Compántas Chorcaí occurred around this time. We did *Campbell of Kylemore* as an Irish contribution to the festival, because Galway was very much in the Gaelic centre. We had a very enjoyable and profitable weekend.

THE QUEEN'S UNIVERSITY OF BELFAST

DRAMATIC SOCIETY

3rd April, 1951.

UNIVERSITIES' DRAMATIC ASSOCIATION.

CUP FOR BEST ACTOR.

Presented to MR. D. DONOVAN for his
performance as "Noah" in the U.D.A.
Festival, Galway, February 1951.

With the compliments of the
Queen's University Dramatic Society.

Dan Donovan's Best Actor Award, 1951.

*Given your passionate interest in theatre, did you ever seriously hesitate
about the teaching?*

No. My life was ploughing merrily along. I was teaching and doing
lots of theatre work with PTG. I was doing a bit of broadcasting.
When the Cork station of Radio Éireann was being formed I got
the job of director. But Seán Ó Tuama said to me: 'You'll be dead
in a year from the drink.' From my own point of view there was too
much going on in Cork. I'd be turning my back on a lot of what I'd

been doing. The job would involve a lot of administration. I don't think Seán thought that was my bag. And if I was working in Radio Éireann I would be susceptible to being moved out of Cork. All in all I wouldn't be in control of my destiny. Seán Mac Reamoinn who died in January 2007 came down and did the job for a year – Síle Ní Bhriain and Máire Ní Mhurchú followed him. Máire contributed a great deal over the years.

Radio Éireann were very ready to broadcast plays of reasonable standard. I remember for one of my first broadcasts I was working with the Little Theatre Society and Eddie Golden in a short version – a very short version; it was half an hour – of *Romeo and Juliet*. I played Mercutio.

By the early 1950s, Compántas Chorcaí was becoming a well-established company. That slow process of development occurred because of Seán's ambitions to write plays of modern interest and techniques in the Irish language. He wanted to get away from the pig-in-the-kitchen, old-fashioned rural play. The Scottish play *Campbell of Kylemore* which we did in translation as part of the University Drama festival in Galway was subsequently broadcast by Radio Éireann, I presume in the old Women's Gaol in Sunday's Well, where much of the broadcasting was done. Geraldine Neeson was the piano accompanist. She had been taught the piano by Frau Tilly Fleischmann, and was very accomplished. She was an all-rounder and as I say a prime force in Cork theatre from the 1920s. Seán, in charge of the studio for years, had been interned in the Women's Gaol during the Troubles!

Geraldine acted in, directed and broadcast B. G. MacCarthy's *The Whip Hand*[25] – an excellent satirical comedy, very sharp and very amusing. I helped to stage-manage the broadcast. *The Whip Hand* helped the Little Theatre Society to keep going. It was revived many times. Seán Healy, who worked in Piggott's music shop near the

Statue [of Fr Mathew on Patrick Street], was in it and Eddie Golden. Eddie played the amusing part of the egg tester. It was a satire on the government creating jobs for their relations. It went out live.

So with your teaching career confirmed early in life you were able to develop many other interests. Was it before or during College that you got interested in sailing?

In fact that happened during College. A friend of mine had a little centre keel yacht and sometime around 1945 or 1946 I spent nearly the whole summer crewing on the dinghy with Frank McDonald. He kept his boat at Boatclub in Blackrock. He was studying to become a radio officer, an option that attracted a lot of people then. The school was down in Tivoli, I think. Whenever we had a bit of time we'd head off. We had a rather nice start, leaving Boatclub and sailing down the river to Cobh or Crosshaven or wherever there was a bit of action, a regatta or a race. I became very taken with sailing and with all the ins and outs of the harbour which I got to know very well. The geography of the harbour became like the back of a book to me. The dinghy had a drop keel so if you went aground all you had to do was lift keel and return to deeper water. That was a grand summer. That summer one of the things I discovered was the great camaraderie of the waterfront. I made lifelong friends who were united in the joy of sailing and pottering around on boats. It wasn't so fashionable in those days. The fleet consisted of all kinds of boats from dinghies and cruisers but nothing like the fleets you have now. There were a few big yachts. Tom and Denis Doyle the stevedores, the Crosbies, and Sam Thompson of Thompson's Bakery had yachts. Joe Fitzgerald of Fitzgerald's menswear shop on 24 Patrick Street had one and the Cudmore brothers had three. A large number of the sailing fraternity were legal. Donal McClement and Joe Kavanagh were members of the legal profession. Even though I wasn't yet a member of the Royal

Munster Yacht Club as it was at the time, in those halcyon days you could use the facilities without paying the fees. I became a life member eventually.

One of the people who was in fact in a class of mine when I returned to Pres in 1947, Jim Collins, became a lifelong friend and boating partner. He was getting into yachting. He bought a dinghy known as *The Nomad*. One of our publican friends named it *The Submarine*. It was of some vintage and it leaked a little. You would see it coming up the river, the mast hardly visible on the horizon. We became partners and bought a dinghy in better condition, called *The Ballyrush*. It was made by Skinners of Baltimore before the invasion of the more popular eighteen-foot dinghies. We'd race in a class that was called Miscellaneous, 'Misc' as we called it. From the Club – which I joined in 1958 – we went to every regatta and race that was available in the harbour. The old Royal Munster was a very welcoming place. Maybe sometimes during the summer you'd get evening sails. You were always welcome as crew. You were at sea at weekends and as much as you wanted. We quickly graduated onto a small cruiser called *The White Tern* and then twelve years later became the owners of *The Blue Tern*, formerly owned by Stanley Roche of Roches Stores and by Cashel Riordan. They were timber boats of a fair vintage. *The White Tern* was built in 1907 and *The Blue Tern* was built in Scotland in 1912. What afterwards became a problem, the maintaining of those boats, was not a problem then because you had many shipwrights in the area. Fibreglass boats had not come in and when they did, the shipwrights became an endangered species. Sailing around the harbour became more popular and extensive from the 1960s on, when fibreglass was in the ascendancy. Fibreglass boats were made in moulds and did not require the exercise of the shipwrights' skill. There was a peculiarly happy atmosphere in the wooden boats, which were very heavy. The Bushe family were great shipwrights. Danny

Pierse was another. There'd be some in Cobh. My boats, all being old, required considerable maintenance during the winter. They were kept in Jackie Keating's boatyard in Crosshaven. I dealt with him until shortly before his death in the late 1970s or early 1980s.

With the two *Terns* we cruised in West Cork waters every summer. The going down and the coming up were a great joy. We made use of every hostelry on the way. We might dally for a day in Kinsale, sail around the Old Head, on to Courtmacsherry, then round the Galley to Glandore and Union Hall and Castlehaven. We felt we were at home when we arrived in Roaring Water Bay, particularly Schull, where we found a very welcoming waterhole in the East End Hotel with the O'Driscolls. Our biggest joy of all was our annual visits to Cape Clear, where we had a deep and lasting friendship with the Burke brothers. Paddy Burke, a big man with a big heart, extended a warm Gaelic welcome to us on Cape Clear every year.

As time went on the Pope family developed the Calves regatta in Schull. On various days during the holiday season in August regattas were held in all parts from Baltimore and Crookhaven. The racing was almost informal then. It was an excuse to go from place to place, in convoy almost. Even while my work in theatre was very active with James N. from 1960 nearly up to 1980, I insisted every year in keeping a fortnight clear for my cruise to West Cork. It's sad to look back on all the warm welcomes everywhere. It's got a little bit commercial. A lot of those we knew are no longer in the hospitality business. I certainly would find it very changed.

There was an advantage that I'm delighted with in my old age – the bungalow. We rented a bungalow in Myrtleville with five or six others for the summer seasons. It was called 'Pearly Gates', a sad misnomer as it was not very pearly, nor very sanctimonious. The Long family with whom we were very friendly over the years rented it to us. It became a kind of annexe to Bunny Connellan's, a great watering hole in Myrtleville. The habit grew up of moving from Bunny's when it closed and carrying crates of beer to 'Pearly Gates'. I remember on one occasion there was an objection to the noise emanating from our bungalow after Bunny's closed. The neighbour objecting was yanked into our shack in his pyjamas, a bottle of beer put in his hand by Michael Powell and told 'Enjoy yourself'.

Unfortunately circumstances caught up with me because of James N. Healy's theatrical tours. I was away from the rented bungalow for quite long periods during the summer. The place got a bit out of control. After a longish tour, I think it was of *Many Young Men of Twenty*, I came back to find the little garden in front of the bungalow almost blotting out the house with a great sea of bottles. I decided there wasn't much future in this. I decided to find a place for myself. My dear old friend Jim Collins told me of a bungalow that was empty, next to his family home in Fennell's Bay. His bungalow was called 'Sans Souci' and they had spent their youth down there. A professional gentleman called Loftus Scully had died intestate and I bid for his bungalow at the end of 1963. I still possess it and take great joy in going down there. It's quite a simple place, a little timber bungalow built in the 1920s. Haphazard bungalows like it sprang up between the wars. All around me they are being dismantled and big concrete villas are taking their place. I expect any day to have a preservation order on it. Fennell's Bay still retains its character as it's a little out of the run of the main roads.

'Pearly Gates' didn't have a flush toilet so we were dependent each week or fortnight on a man politely called 'The Honey Man' to visit and clear the toilet. I moved into the lap of luxury with a flush toilet in my new bungalow. But I was sorry to leave 'Pearly Gates'. I was very fond of it. A little thing I found recently reminded me of it, an old Electricity Supply Board [ESB] bill from the early 1960s which said 'This account is now closed.'

I suppose in those post-war winters it was back to the city where theatre and music took over?

Yes. In the Little Theatre Society I had become friends with Eddie Golden whom I found an invaluable mentor. He was an extremely good actor and generous with advice that was full of common sense and practicality. I played Flingsley the schoolmaster in Paul Vincent Carroll's *Shadow and Substance,* a professional production with Eddie in the old Opera House in 1948. I think after that production Eddie went to the Abbey where he stayed for the rest of his life.

In 1952 I played in James Stack's production of Walter Macken's *Home is the Hero*, his play about Galway life which was adapted for the cinema in Ardmore Studios.

That was the only time I played with Jim as an actor. Jim in the 1930s spent some years in the United States and attended drama school with the famous American actor Burgess Meredith. Possibly

Dan Donovan and Gretta Sexton, **Home is the Hero,** *1952.*

because of the almost total concentration on Shakespeare in the Loft, Eddie and Jim and indeed some others got a bit restive. As a matter of temperament I myself found Fr O'Flynn overwhelming. He had a powerful face and very penetrating eyes. He was authoritarian. There is a very pathetic account of him waiting for Stackie and Eddie Golden to come back to the Loft. In fact they never went back. Eddie and Jim Stack and indeed Geraldine were very important figures in the development of the LTS, which mounted productions of a high standard of modern and Shakespearean plays in the old Opera House. They took it in turns to direct and while the LTS was essentially amateur, there was a small fee for the director of the plays. This was to cause some jostling for position and a little touch of rivalry, which led to further developments and changes in time. Eddie and Jim were both good actors. Jim was a little limited in the sense of his appearance – he was tall and his dark piercing eyes and concentrated gaze made him for many people a formidable figure. That would have limited his range as an actor in some ways. But he was probably one of the best directors that Cork ever turned out. Jim could be quite hypnotic in his effect on people. The eyes and that stare could reduce you to a frazzle. Eddie was a more lyrical and wide-ranging actor but perhaps not as imaginative a director as Jim. I think an incipient rivalry developed between them. In hindsight I suppose it was no great surprise when Jim left the LTS to form a production company of his own – James Stack Productions. This inflicted a severe blow on the LTS who lost an important actor and director.

In the early 1930s Jim became the first holder of a full-time post in Speech and Drama in the Cork School of Music, run by the VEC. There followed an extraordinary number of splendid productions and performances. His choice of repertoire was often dictated by the commercial needs of the Opera House but he told me that every year the production in the School of Music would be chosen to give the class experience of plays of the highest quality. He cultivated techniques of voice production and acting of the highest standard. He trained a very, very distinguished company of actors. He worked professionally of course. He paid his cast and was able to recruit many of his most successful pupils in the Drama class in the School of Music. For instance Michael McAuliffe, one of our best actors, was a product of that. And Lorna Daly, who like Fr O'Flynn could cure people of their stammers. Theatre-goers of the older generation will recall people like Eddie Mulhare who made a career in Hollywood. He was in the TV series *The Ghost and Mrs Muir*. When I met him on a visit to Cork in the early 1970s through the Film Festival, he was enthusiastic about Jim Stack's skills as a teacher and director. Bill O'Brien was another actor who subsequently went professional and also went to America, where he died rather prematurely. Though in many ways Jim and I became rivals when I became involved in production companies myself, we remained close friends and often after classes in the School of Music we had long chats. He seemed almost a permanent fixture in the world of Cork theatre and his sudden death in 1973 left a void. His marriage had broken down. He was turning the key to enter his flat in Douglas when he dropped dead. The void he left was gradually filled by some of his former students – Rosemary Archer, Máirín Prendergast [née Murphy], and Abbey Scott, who had trained in RADA. I did a lot of work with Abbey and all of them over the years. Abbey married Charlie Hennessy, a former Pres student and a great patron of Cork theatre and the arts in general.

Was a Jim Stack panto being rehearsed when the old Opera House burnt down?

Yes, it was – the Christmas panto. The night of the fire [12 December 1955] I was in the Vineyard, one of my ports of call in those days. Lots of ex-College people were there. There was a poets' corner, as we called it, at one end. Seán Ó Ríordáin used often be there until he got himself barred. Liam Mackesy, owner of the Vineyard, was a very kindly man but something must have happened. Seán Ó Ríordáin wasn't too far from us growing up in Ballincollig. I got to know him coming in on the bus. He'd be going up to the Mon and I'd be dumped off at the Western Road for Pres. I also knew him because my aunt Lell was a great friend of Miss Linehan, his aunt who had a little shop up the steps at Iniscarra. The existence of Jacky Riordan was indeed well known to me as a boy. The Vineyard had great atmosphere and a great bar man, Bill Shea – tall, thin, discreet – the best filler of a pint who ever lived. I'd drink any stout but Bill was a supreme maker of Guinness. He'd use three barrels, half fill the pint glass with one, then another and finally use the third high barrel to give a delicious top. You waited, knowing that a work of art was being prepared. In the middle of this, on that fateful Tuesday, someone rushed in and said 'Boys, the Opera House has gone up. It's blazing.' However attractive Bill's pints were, off we went across to Emmet Place. It was one of the wettest nights God ever sent Cork and God knows he sent a lot of them. By the time we got there, despite the best efforts of the rain and the fire brigade, the place was alight. I remember I and others were close to Booth and Fox's, the mattress manufacturers opposite the Opera House entrance. We were gazing across at what was the end of the Opera House as we knew it.

The panto cast was rehearsing under Jim. They were coming out on to the streets. They had smelt smoke all during the rehearsals. A lot of the staff were in that night – Ned Allen, Michael Scannell and Christy Props. They were looking on as their jobs went up in smoke. I couldn't tell you what Christy's real name was. He was in charge of properties. Jars. Cups. Things for the stage sets. He was the go-getter who had them in stock in his little room, or acquired them. Billa O'Connell,[26] our great comedian, was recently married and had to tell his wife that the prospect of their suite of furniture was gone up in smoke. The panto would run for six weeks and was financially important to the theatre.

There was a short circuit between the ceiling and the roof in the auditorium. Of course it must have been starting slowly for a while. No cause was found. There was a lot of old timber and rubber felting there. It was like a tinder-box. It couldn't have been worse – it was the perfect bonfire. The old carpets and furniture were so full of character but not good for an emergency of that kind. The fire brigade were working like hell but the odds were against them. The fire was spreading. We were very emotional. It was a very popular old building. It had acquired so much history and memory. The old Athenaeum, as it originally was, had been a cultural hall where Charles Dickens gave recitals of his work. It was a lovely theatre, pleasantly dilapidated, full of smells and warm human qualities. Bill Twomey, the manager, had succeeded John Daly. John had been a Christian Brother, left and came back to Cork as manager of the Opera House and had brought business back to the Opera House through hard, imaginative grafting. Bill Twomey would have been broadening that – English companies were coming back. All this was coming to a full stop, not only for the panto, but for all the local musical societies, the Cork Operatic Society, The Gilbert and Sullivan Society and others.

The Opera House was a very important part of Irish touring. Not only was this a blow to Cork, it was a blow to the entire theatrical profession in Ireland, especially as John Daly had done such a magnificent job during the War keeping the Opera House going with Irish talent. Next stop would be Cork for Jimmy O'Dea as soon as he finished the panto or one of their revues in the Gaiety. All the Dublin seasons of both the Lord Longford and the Mac Liammóir and Edwards productions in the Gate were replicated in Cork. There was a whole world going up in flames. The Abbey had gone up in flames four years earlier.

The memories were flying. The cast of *Sleeping Beauty* were on the street from the nearby dance studios. It was like a living history of theatre in Cork, listening to the memories being recalled. The roof was beginning to go. The heat was coming across the street. We had to move away. The climax of the evening in the rain and darkness and vivid blaze was the great theatrical gesture which came from the House itself – the moment when the roof fell in. You could almost feel it as a physical thing. Here was the burning roof coming down on the seats. It was almost as if a living thing was being destroyed before our eyes.

Then the fire brigade were able to get on top of the flames. Once the roof was gone they could douse the burning areas inside. We stayed until one or half past. We couldn't tear ourselves away. We eventually did tear ourselves away, with a huge void in our lives.

Crowds watch as the Opera House burns down, 12 December 1955.

5

Working with Seán Ó Tuama

What was Ireland like in the early to mid 1950s, before the programme for economic recovery and the opening up to America and the Continent was manifest?

While the War was awful, with its rationing, the 'glimmer' of gas, the half-ounce of tea and the shortage of clothes, it meant that people had to be as careful as possible about everything. While we basically had enough to eat in Ireland, it was true that every unfortunate crow was shot and de-feathered to send to England, where the food need was dire. The jokes in Ireland were all about the Irish rail system, where it was alleged that people had to get out of the trains to collect pieces of turf and sticks to stoke the engines. The capacity to improvise was always necessary.

Patty was a wonderful forager. In Dunmanway, she would manage to contrive to get an extra ounce of tea now and again, to help the family here. Towards the end of the War, Tim married in Wales. On her visits to Wales on the old *Inisfallen,* Patty would always bring butter and whatever else she could forage for the young family there. I was very aware of clothes rationing because on the occasion of one of the public debates in College, I became very self-conscious about the poor quality of my shirt. I borrowed some coupons from my aunt Kit and from Betty to avoid that happening again. While the 1940s were in a way rather self-regarding and stifling, in a sense all this effort to survive and provide ourselves with the necessities of life stood us in very good stead when times began to turn around in the 1950s. We gained expertise in drama for example through the festivals and through John Daly using the local companies and the Dublin professional companies.

I rarely understand people who run down the 1950s. I found the 1950s encouraging. Things were obviously better than they had been. Being young, the only possibilities we entertained were that things would get better. There were gradual signs of prosperity. We had quite a decent trade surplus by the end of the War. We were selling more to England than we were buying. Rationing declined and a new sort of hope and trust in ourselves, which had in fact developed in the bad days, developed.

One knows all that's said about the rigidities of the Church and the Irish class system. Our sense was that with the new dynamic in society, things would change and, having survived the War, we would be able to change them. I think this personal feeling was matched by a general governmental sense that things had to get better. Thinking went on in high places. It was certainly thinking, because there was no money. The dream was that with our huge resources in scenery and with the foundations laid by the Literary Revival and the new cultural nationalism, opportunities could be furthered, using the cultural expertise that had developed at local levels during the War. Local and national interests began to combine in all sorts of ways, leading to features like *An Tóstal* [The Pageant].

An Tóstal was discussed thoroughly in 1952–3 and partially planned on a national scale by Seán Lemass, who had a strong sense that Ireland needed to be opened up after the rigours and rigidities of wartime restrictions. It seemed that the best way to do this was to establish a series of festivals all over Ireland, which would extend the tourist season into early summer and autumn. In 1953 *An Tóstal*, the Festival of Cork, got under way.

An Tóstal was a kind of a holdall bag during its early years. I remember at one of the early *Tóstals*, Benjamin Britten and Peter Pears gave a recital in the School of Music under the auspices of the Cork Orchestral Society. It was packed. It was a marvellous recital. It meant that international figures were to become an increasingly familiar sight on our stages and in our concert halls.

In this national movement Cork was fortunate in that the artistic and organisational skills of Der Breen were recognised and utilised. He became director of *An Tóstal*. I was in charge of drama. Der's gift for friendship and organisation came into play once more. He tended to use a network of friends with whom he got on well and worked well. He would say to me 'Dan, is there anything available of a suitable standard and nature that wouldn't cost money that we could do for *An Tóstal*?' 'Ann' we used to call 'her'. 'What are we doing for 'Ann' this year?' we'd say. I would find something usually. The dramatic contributions went on until the early 1960s.

Had Der given up the job as a commercial traveller then?

He had. He had a good physical base in Cork because he had secured the job of manager of the Palace cinema on MacCurtain Street. It wasn't only a cinema, it was a lovely old music hall theatre. When the Opera House burnt down, Der was only too anxious to open his doors to the Cork companies who were totally dejected by its loss.

Since An Tóstal *was an idea favoured by government, and the Arts Council had just been founded, was there not a budget?*

In the first two years there was a bit of a budget available to us from the Arts Council.[27] The Presentation Group and Geraldine Neeson put on two plays each in the Opera House for *An Tóstal* one year.

The old Palace cinema,15 MacCurtain Street, Cork.

Another year we revived the Famine play, *The Black Stranger* by Gerard Healy. We also did *The Wise Have Not Spoken* by Paul Vincent Carroll. Our slender budget was expended on getting a professional director, Seamus Breathnach, from Radio Éireann for that.

There was hassle because Presentation Theatre Guild couldn't go in with our own name as we were amateur. I think we were called the Cork Arts Society or something of that kind for the purposes of *An Tóstal*. There was a programme of four one-act plays in the Pres theatre during one *Tóstal*. We put on *In the Shadow of the Glen* by Synge ourselves. Rachel Burrows did *The Words upon the Window Pane*, Yeats's play about Swift. Bill Mahony, the well-known director who ran the Well Players, put on *The Pipe in the Fields* by T. C. Murray. *Michelmas Eve* by T. C. Murray was directed by Bill another year, in the Catholic Young Men's Society [CYMS]. It had the indigenous element which was part of the *Tóstal* policy.

Was the theatre in Presentation College a key venue, especially when the Opera House was lost?

The Western Road school was extended in the early 1950s. Part of this new wing could be turned into a nice, small-sized theatre. One room was designed to be a stage without losing its function for class purposes. With the judicious use of folding doors it could easily be converted into a theatre. Raymond Kelleher was the architect. It was able to contain moderately elaborate productions. It was a very useful space. The Pres Group had our own scene man, the late Bill Coughlan, and our own electrician. All functions were looked after in an effective way. The generosity of the school meant that we had the space for nothing. We did not pay for heat or light. You can imagine the lighting costs. We would be able to put on something like *Murder in the Cathedral* because we'd have done a comedy earlier on and there'd be something in the kitty. You'd plan it that way. The understanding was that you'd finance your own productions. Local organisations like the Presentation Order were contributors to the policy of having good plays but there was no way of getting subsidies when you had the word 'amateur' constantly used against you in a pejorative way.

After the two years when we did get the subsidy there were questions, and subsequent productions, apart from Seán Ó Tuama's *Gunna Cam agus Slabhra Óir,* were less ambitious. When Arts Council subsidies ceased or became minimal we were still able to persuade groups to present theatrical productions for *An Tóstal.* As far as I can tell the last drama contribution to *An Tóstal* was Seán Ó Tuama's *Is é seo m'Oileán/This is my Island,* his play about the servant girl with the baby, where the master of the house, a businessman in Cork, wants her out. It was a nice ironic title. Any thing that ruffled feathers was grist to Seán's mill.

One of the highlights of *An Tóstal* in 1957 was the first Cork production of Seán's play *Gunna Cam agus Slabhra Óir.* The president of Ireland, Seán T. Ó Ceallaigh, visited Cork specially for this production.[28] It was in the School of Music. Conversation after the play

Seán Ó Tuama, President Seán T. Ó Ceallaigh, Dan Donovan, 30 May 1957.

was very lively. We gave him a few balls of his favourite ten-year-old Jameson and things livened up.

The Crooked Gun and the Golden Chain/Gunna Cam agus Slabhra Óir is a metaphor depicting the twin strands of violence and negotiation that are still relevant in the Irish tradition. The *slabhra óir* is in the ascendent at the moment. The *gunna cam* has slipped back. The swing between the two polarities is something that has long been a feature in Irish politics. Do you talk or do you fight? It was a play of Shakespearean range where the powerful central dilemma is worked through to the very end, with the deposing and imprisonment of Mánas. He is the leading character, one of the talkers or negotiators and is replaced by his more revolutionary son Calbhac. That might seem a rather broad confrontation but the play is richly worked out, with devices like the Fool and the long meditative reflections of an t-Athair Eoghan, which lend powerful philosophical comment to the central dilemma of the play. I was double-jobbing – I played Mánas – I suppose Mánas was written for me – and directed. We had Niall Toibín as an tAthair Eoghan and Seamus Ó Tuama, Seán's cousin, as the Fool. The company which we formed to do the plays, Compántas Chorcaí, was reinforced for the production by these two Dublin guests. Well, Niall is very much a Cork man.

Gunna Cam was the second of Seán's two verse plays. Not all of Seán's plays were first produced in the School of Music. A number were done in Dublin first. It was written in Paris and premiered in the Abbey. Seán Ó Riada wrote a score for the Abbey production. The Cork productions were often enabled by some of the costs being absorbed by a Dublin production. There would be very good support from audiences. That was amazing.

Yes, it does now seem amazing. Audiences have different imaginations now, maybe. What were Seán's politics?

Seán's politics would have been very Fianna Fáil. He wrote fluently and easily in Irish. He did feel that the language to which he was devoted was best protected by the Fianna Fáil tradition.

You were saying he was very European in his approach to theatre?

He was. In France he would have come across Armand Salacrou and the existential questioning that was very much part of the post-war scene in Paris. He was strongly academic. His varied methods of attack, as it were, showed an extraordinary range.[29]

How did you bring on your own Irish?

I was going to do Irish in my degree when I went to UCC in 1944 but I found it an extraordinarily dreary business. I think I was driven out of honours and then I did the pass and I found it absolutely mind-bogglingly boring. It was very dead and mechanical.

Mechanical lectures were read out. I did five subjects in first arts and Irish was in my view the dreariest of the five. I abandoned even pass Irish for my degree. Later I had a major job bringing my Gaelic skills back. I had left Gaelic behind in some disgust. It was dry and academic. When I was brushing up my Irish I used to go to Kerry every year. Seán Ó Ríordáin would go to Ballyferriter. I'd meet him there regularly. Seán Ó Tuama used be down there as well. I always stayed at Dún Cíobháin in Ballyferriter, where the owner, Seán Ó Cíobháin, was a great friend and teacher.

Seán Ó Tuama came at things actively in a living way. He was a very good critic and wrote a splendid book, *An Grá in Amhráin na nDaoine* (1960), on how courtly love poetry survived in folk literature. It was a huge work of scholarship to which he devoted some years. He also edited *An Duanaire 1600–1900: Poems of the Dispossessed* (1981) with Thomas Kinsella. He wrote a very good book, *Filí faoi Sceimhle: Seán Ó Ríordáin agus Aogán Ó Rathaille* (1978), in which he takes two poets of a different period, Seán Ó Ríordáin and Aogán Ó Rathaille, the eighteenth-century Kerry poet, and links these poets under pressure in an interesting, counterpointed study. The historical background comes into play in each case: in Ó Rathaille's case, the scholarly poet in eighteenth-century Anglicised Ireland and in Seán Ó Ríordáin's, the struggle with ill-health in a modern Ireland. Seán Ó Tuama by his critical skills helped to establish the stature of Seán Ó Ríordáin as a major poet. He brought him into UCC to do some teaching in his latter days. Seán Ó Ríordáin's relationship with Corkery would have been more critical than Seán Ó Tuama's. Corkery had gone off the boil and Seán Ó Tuama gave Corkery's seminal ideas a living relevance. It was quite an extraordinary period of artistic ferment. Seán Ó Riada, who was a little after me in College, was one of the figures of that sort of ferment. He had also left the scene and gone to the Continent, before taking up Seán Neeson's job teaching Irish music on Seán's retirement from UCC in 1963. He was trying to do the same thing – making an effort to bring Irish classical music, not folk, into the forms that were coming into vogue. He was interested in how that might depend on the rich vein of traditional music that he developed with Ceoltóirí Cualann, who ultimately became the Chieftains.

Did you and Seán Ó Tuama work together until the early 1970s, a relatively stable period in the economic and cultural life of Cork city?

Yes. In the seven other plays, Seán experimented with very imaginative and lively content in a serious effort to find new and innovative methods of staging. The eight plays represented an extraordinary range. For example *Moloney* (1956), his first one-act play in Irish, dealt with the interrogation of Oliver Plunkett in Drogheda where a drunken priest Moloney was being brainwashed into giving evidence at the subsequent trial. I played Moloney and directed. Seán really used the methods of interrogation and techniques of intimidation that the Nazis had used – 'Ve have vays of making you talk'. All this made the seventeenth century come alive in terms of twentieth-century awareness. It was put on first in the School of Music on Union Quay and then in the Damer in Dublin. It was revived during the second Everyman season in the Catholic Young Men's Society theatre in Castle Street. That would have been 1964.

Ar Aghaidh Linn, a Longadáin (1959) probably represents my favourite. It deals with the so-often treated theme of Mad Sweeney who descends into the Kingdom of Labhra Loinsigh which is devastated and rendered barren by a false devotion to wrong-headed Science. Mad Sweeney re-introduces sanity, joy and poetry. It's a wonderfully spontaneous play. I adored playing Sweeney and I adored every moment of the production. It was full of exuberant language and full of colour and has a very important message: we dare not neglect the instinctive, creative part of man. If I were to resurrect anything from my past, my sinful past, I would cheerfully play Mad Sweeney again.

Is é seo m'Oileán/ This is my Island, was more Ibsenite. It attacked the smugness of the middle classes. The serving girl who has had a baby out of wedlock comes into conflict with various attitudes in a rather stolid, middle-class family. The livelier side of that play were the women. They reflected the range of options the central character posed. Some of our regular actors were teachers. The teachers were a godsend for keeping those things going – the old time factor was always there. Máire Nic Lochlainn affectionately known as Locky and Eibhlín Ní Drisceoil and Máire Ní Shé were regulars among others who were available from time to time. It wasn't necessarily the kind of play that was very common at the time, 1961. I was the father. I was a 'heavy', as they say; ponderous, smug, middle class, altogether different to the madness of Sweeney. Its first public performance was in the School of Music for *The Tóstal* in 1961. I still have the brochure.

Seán had changed tack for another play, *Ceist ar Phádraig/Queries for Patrick* (1960), which we did in the School of Music – we were tied up with the Irish drama class of the School of Music where the VEC support was invaluable. It was a revue-type play with music and song in which the traditional Church and the more modern, trendier aspects of religion were contrasted. A rather bothered St Patrick was trying to deal with a world that was very alien to him. It was a lively romp. Inevitably I played St Patrick. The contrast with him was Blessed Martin de Porres, the black saint from the West Indies, the pop saint as it were, the handsome, fashionable, black man. The Vatican recommendations were very much in the air and there was a sort of ferment that led to fears about changes that might be controversial or difficult but felt by many to be necessary.

I was particularly conscious of this as a member of the St Augustine Church Choir in the centre of the city, because we had the changes to the vernacular in the Church services. For instance Latin would play a much smaller role, a minimal role, in Church services. As someone who had an honours degree in Latin that bothered me. It interfered with my own educational direction. It would affect me in a lot of ways. I didn't do modern languages in school as Latin – and Greek if you wanted it – was the pillar of the curriculum. I taught some Latin in Pres, but oddly enough not as much as I expected to, for purely practical reasons of staff balance. I have to confess that the sense of change in this case unsettled me a bit. The tradition was part of me and my growing up. As a result I didn't continue with the choir. It was quite a good choir and there were a range of motets principally sung in Latin and many four-part Masses that I loved. High Mass with celebrant, deacon and subdeacon all on the altar and the vestments and incense and all the paraphernalia of those days made the celebration a very artistic thing. We were spoiled with the richness and the range of the traditional ritual. Now the poor priest struggles along alone. The triumphalism mercifully has gone.

At that time I was facing problems finding time to rehearse with the choir. The changes in my world of theatre meant I had less leisure time. When I left the choir I felt the loss of something I had been doing for over twenty years. I had started in school. Der Breen was with me in the choir as a classmate. His brother Brendan, having come home from the Capuchins where he had been a seminarian, had his basic degree but he had to do his Higher Diploma to undertake a teaching career and earn his crust. During the period of his renewed university education he got the job of director of the choir – he had the Church music. The new Augustinian Church was being rebuilt around the remaining fabric of the older church on Grand Parade and Washington Street. The big modern Romanesque Church went up in place of the humbler Gothic one. The great thing in those days was that people tended to drive into the city as a kind of occasion to go to Mass on Sundays. The full congregation you'd have in St Augustine's would be reflected in St Francis' Church on Liberty Street or in St Peter and Paul's. All three churches were within a stone's throw of one another. The twelve o'clock Mass with all its trappings was the packed one. The suburbanites would drive in to that in all their finery.

Speaking about visual spectacle, who would do the sets for Ó Tuama's plays?

Pat MacSweeney, who was the architect who designed the County Hall skyscraper on the Lee Road, gave his time and talent to our settings. He was a man of quick understanding and great imagination. His talents made a wonderful contribution to the presentation of the plays. He and Seán – and we all – sparked off one another. There was a kind of imaginative frisson between the three of us – through the writing, the acting and the setting. *Corp Eoghan Uí Shúilleabháin* (1963) would have been Seán's fifth or sixth play. It was written in two acts with two interludes. The movements of the play were given musical titles – allegro, scherzo and andante. The setting he wanted was such as would be done by Salvador Dali. In a very big cast there was one living person, Eoghan Uí Shúilleabháin himself. It was very surreal, very imaginative. I'm not too sure that the 'dead' cast were always too sure about what was going on. We used the music of *Der Mond/The Moon* by Carl Orff, the *Carmina Burana* man.

I think we did five of Seán's plays in the School of Music and three with revivals in the Young Men's. In the Young Men's in Castle Street in 1967 Everyman did *Judas Iscariot agus a Bhean*, Seán's play which linked the mental breakdown in the actor playing Judas with the character of Judas in the play. The artistic elements and the realistic ones are counterpointed. The character he is playing and the ordinary actor's human situation are intertwined. I found the production and playing of this very original. He used the interlude formula again. I remember more than any of the previous plays he worked on it a good deal during the Cork run. I remember being handed a few pages of interludes as he called them in which he commented non-realistically on the events of the central theme of the play, the mental breakdown of Judas. I was Judas. I found it exhausting. It was most demanding, mainly because of the shifts of level in the play.

Alas my weariness may have been a factor in it but I was reluctant to attempt Seán's next play. *Déan Trócaire ar na Sagairt Óga/Have Pity on the Young Priests* is a play in a series of episodes in which Seán explores the problems facing a young priest in the new Ireland, in which the theme of homosexuality was brought out very cleverly. Michael Davitt, Nuala Ní Dhomhnaill and Bob Crowley played in it. Frank Fitzgerald did the set. I didn't in fact direct it. Tomás Ó Murchú, a promising young director whose career was cut short by an untimely death within a year or two, directed. Seán prevailed upon me to take the part of Mícheál an Taxi in the play. So I acted a very powerful and poetic cameo part of a tormented older man whose basic tenderness of soul is blocked. He does a brutal thing: he destroys a poor little bird accidentally in one sombre scene.

That was sadly the last of Seán's plays. Seán and I understood one another so well after all the years. We were a little bit defeated by the difficulties. The basic team of Compántas Chorcaí was quite hard worked. While we were both born in the same year – 1926 – the factor of aging in my case was becoming significant. Our resources were few. There was the constant difficulty of getting good actors who had enough good Irish. Seán would be able to see what was around the University in any given year. That was a great help. He may have felt he had gone as far as he could in the eight plays.

Dermot Crowley and Dan Donovan in Seán Ó Tuama's Déan Trócaire ar na Sagairt Óga.

All the investment of hard work had insufficient wider fruit. He translated *Judas* into English and was bitterly disappointed with the quality of his translation. He told me it came out like *Peig's Paper* – in other words his own feeling for the Irish language was what worked for him. It was trivialised in English. Seán wanted to do everything possible to further the welfare and defence of the Irish language.

Would it be true to say that there seem to have been a lot of plays with priests in them written in the pre-Vatican II period? I was just noticing an old Opera House poster advertising Mrs Louis D'Alton in A Priest *for example.*

There were several plays about priests. For example Paul Vincent Carroll, a national school teacher whose play I was mentioning earlier – *Shadow and Substance* – had considerable trouble with his clerical manager and a great deal of his output dealt with the conflicts that arose. He made very successful use of that conflict in *Shadow and Substance*. In Eddie Golden's production in the old Opera House in 1948 I was the schoolteacher pitted against the central character, the Canon. Subsequently I had the pleasure of playing the Canon in the first full-length, Irish language performance of *Shadow and Substance,* which Compántas Chorcaí put on; it was an An Gúm translation edited by Seán to ensure it conformed to the Munster dialect. The Canon was trying to practise nepotism in that he wanted to appoint a niece of his to a position in the school. That was very common. Nuns for example would quite often employ a lay teacher on a temporary basis until such time as a nun became available to teach. Then the temporary teacher would be let go. Those were the days of plenty of vocations. Paul Vincent Carroll was one of the best known dramatists from the 1930s to the 1950s and the first very well known playwright of the period to deal with the collision between lay and secular interests. Through that he developed into wider areas of conflict.

That there was sometimes continuous conflict or unease was something I knew from my own house, because my mother as a national school teacher had some degree of conflict with the religious management of the school. For instance one manager, Fr Sexton, a man who was partial to a little drink, was very anti the Irish language. One year – I would say in the early 1930s – a letter containing Irish arrived from the Department of Education. He threw the whole lot into the fire. Unfortunately the letter happened to contain the cheque for winter fuel for the school. My mother at her own expense had to go to John Boyd in the village of Ballincollig and ask him to supply the fuel. In those days quite a few of the children had bare feet. There were old iron stoves in the school, which had been a church, and they were insufficient to warm the place in the very cold weather. My mother of course was reimbursed by the Department.

On another occasion a priest came examining the children in catechism and demanded the rattan, the stick, from my mother in order to punish wrong answers. 'Fetch the rattan' he said. 'Under no circumstances am I going to allow you or any stranger to punish children in this school. That's a duty totally reserved to me,' she said. That was the end of that. She wasn't a woman to be argued with. Fr Sexton wouldn't be one of those looking for the rattan. He was rather grand. He wouldn't demean himself. Fr Sexton had a brother a priest, Dean Sexton. Dean Sexton was a well-spoken, educated man, sitting on many cultural committees. At a time when reading the Bible as myth was not at all usual, he'd say 'You can't take everything you read in the Bible literally. I wouldn't give you tuppence for that story of Adam and Eve and the apple.'

He was feared as the diocesan censor of the theatre. If there was anything objectionable in the text, he would take it out. The word went round that you should see the play on the first night. You'd get the full text that night and you might not get it on the second night. There was a strong feeling that the theatre was the Whore of Babylon. There were about four or five priests I knew who liked to attend the Opera House. Ned Allen the electrician, would, with the permission of management, bring them up to the lighting box or seat them just behind the curtain in the wings, so that they would not be seen.

A few decades earlier, there were the priest-novelists like Canon Sheehan who wrote for a mainly Catholic audience, avoiding unsuitable ideas.[30]

Yes. Those books were all in my mother's library in Ballincollig. I remember reading Canon Sheehan's *My New Curate* (1900) and *Glenanaar* (1905) there.

At Ballincollig concerts to raise money, the Dean and Fr Sexton would do duets, old sea songs maybe for tenor and bass. I remember them singing 'The Moon Hath Raised Her Lamp' from *The Lily of*

Killarney, the Dean accompanying on the piano as Fr Sexton, a short, tubby man, took up his position behind the piano.

Fr Sexton would probably get his crate of Jameson from Woodford Bournes in [62-4] Patrick Street, but it couldn't be delivered to the Parochial House. It was sent to Fielding's, the chemists, where it would be repackaged in anything from toilet-paper wrapping to pharmaceutical boxes. It would then go on its merry way, cargo undeclared, to be delivered to the Parochial House.

He was a bit deaf. 'You did *what*!' you'd hear reverberating through the church as people were in the confessional. One day my mother's friend Nonie Shea went in to the box to have her confession heard. Having unburdened herself, Nonie came out. 'Chris' she said to my mother 'there's a terrible smell of Christmas in the box.'

I recall during holidays in Ballycotton a group of female national teachers recounting their various experiences and I must say that I have rarely heard such anti-clerical views as I heard expressed by this group of mature spinsters and the married women among them.

Fascinating.

There were plays, yes, about priests. There was a play which we put on in Theatre of the South, *The Righteous are Bold,* a melodramatic play with good acting parts, in which a priest does an exorcism. There was one from the Ulster Group who toured to the Opera House, called *Is the Priest at Home?* by Joe Tomelty. It was directed by Harold Goldblatt, a good Jew playing a Catholic priest.

Priests emerge in all sorts of ways, largely sentimental. In Carroll's fine study of the Canon in *Shadow and Substance* and in the crippled, easy-going Canon Matt Lavelle in *The White Steed*, in which the young priest is confronted for his narrowness by the more open-minded Canon, trained on the Continent, we see Carroll's searching concern. Carroll's first Abbey play *Things That Are Caesar's* (1932) began his career with a dominating priest. Priests had the power. Paul Vincent Carroll touched closer to the bone than most playwrights then. When Seán Ó Tuama wrote his last play *Have Pity on the Young Priests* in 1969–1970, the discussion on problems sexual and otherwise was sensitive, but fairly oblique.

You played many priest parts over time?

For a John O'Shea Everyman production in the late 1960s I did a cameo part of a Jesuit trying to woo the young James Joyce into the order. It was *Stephen D* by the Dublin dramatist with a wide range of interest, Hugh Leonard. I played every kind of ecclesiastic in my career, from a 'spoilt priest' to a saint. But alas I never succeeded in playing a pope, though I did have a strong ambition to play the part of the pope in Brecht's *The Life of Galileo,* where a genial pope gradually assumes a sense of presence and rigorous authority as he carefully dons the bits and pieces of his papal attire.

What about the maternal vocation?

One of the finest dramatic studies of what was rather carefully referred to as 'the spoilt priest' was *Maurice Harte* (1912) by T. C. Murray.[31] The Abbey took it to London before the First World War, with considerable success. I once directed an Irish translation of this splendid play. Murray took on with a serious and tragic vision some of the more pressing social and psychological problems that were a regular feature of Irish society. A common notion with a moderately well-to-do family was that the elder boy would get the farm and the younger son become a priest or vice versa. Choices were limited. I was conscious of this as my father had to get out of the house in Glandore and join the RIC. I often think I could easily find a parallel with O'Faolain's family situation and my own in this respect. His father was in the RIC and his mother a working mother also.

Religious vocations were very often carefully nurtured by the mother, maybe by both parents, but the vocations wished on the young man by virtue of limited career choices and the fact that it was quite clear to him as he grew up that no way was he going to be left a bit of ground were often referred to as 'mothers' vocations'. Very often the mother desired the mark of spiritual approval that a priest in the family would bring. Very often then a problem would emerge in the seminary. Quite a number might defect as the human pressures became increasingly evident and militated against staying in. Quite often the decision of the young man might be long delayed until the death of the mother whose heart he would not break. Quite often he would remain an unhappy and suffering priest.

6

The Choral and Film Festivals

Right across Europe after the War, festivals became a big thing. You were very involved in Cork festivals, especially the Choral Festival[32] and the Film Festival.

The Film Festival and the Choral Festival are the surviving events of *An Tóstal*. The first International Choral Festival in Cork occurred in 1954. The Film Festival followed in 1956. Theatrically speaking, even though we had some splendid plays during *An Tóstal*, there was an inherent flaw in the *Tóstal* notion of extending the season. Tactically these times of the year, early summer and autumn, were not ideal for drama. Possibly it was good for the tourist season. But theatrically speaking you'd be between seasons.

Was the timing for the Cork International Choral Festival better?

Yes. By contrast the time of the year was perfect for the Choral Festival. The whole climatic thing suited. The snows had melted. The days were getting longer, the evenings brighter and it was easier for choirs to travel. Church choirs were easing off after Easter. I remember a particularly brilliant programme in Fitzgerald's Park. It was just when all the flowers were starting to blossom. I have engraved in my memory the experience of watching and listening to a Czech choir, a ladies' choir. They first sang Mass in the Vincentians in Sunday's Well and moved down over the little footbridge in full costume into Fitzgerald's Park, which was glowing with early summer flowers, singing Czech folk songs as they moved. It was a moment of extraordinary beauty. For a change the weather was good.

The weather killed that programme in Fitzgerald's Park. It was more often raining or showery or bitterly cold. Eventually it disappeared. Singers do not want to sing in the open air when the weather is uncertain, if not downright inclement.

Tell me more about your own role in the Choral Festival.

That reminds me of the appalling pressure I was under as sole presenter of the Choral Festival. That Sunday for example I would have started at ten o'clock with the small choirs in City Hall. I would have got up to Fitzgerald's Park by twelve and presented the programme there. I'd get away from Fitzgerald's Park by 2.15 p.m. Betty used to have my dinner ready here. I'd snatch my dinner and be back in City Hall for 3 p.m. Then followed the gala farewell programme at 7.30 p.m.

I can recall one unscheduled stop. I had a scooter which I fell off on a slippery road. I ripped the knee out of my trousers and grazed my leg. I had to go home and get alternative raiment. Pilib Ó Laoghaire of Cór Cois Laoi stepped into the breach and covered the first two items of the programme until I arrived in a fairly decent state.

The Choral Festival took off out of the blue. Such success wasn't expected. It was felt originally that it would bring in foreign choirs and after the War that seemed an excellent thing to do. It worked splendidly. We had a German choir from Dortmund who won the first Choral Festival. It was very touching. Éamonn Ó Gallchobhair was the Irish adjudicator. The English adjudicator was Leslie

Woodgate of the BBC singers. Here he was in Cork in 1954 giving the chief prize to the German choir. It was a sign of the whole change since the War and of music becoming a language of universal peace. In his speech he very graciously acknowledged the beauty and harmony of the choir from the country of England's former enemy and the role music has in universal peacemaking.

Then we had a splendid choir from Modena, of which Pavarotti's father Fernando was an important member. During the visit of the choir, Pavarotti came down. I think he was singing in Dublin. Some people said he sang in Cork but I didn't notice him: I think I would have noticed him! His father sang a solo with the Modena choir. A lot of people were annoyed that he wasn't asked to repeat it. They were seeking him out. He was a small, stocky man, a baker, very popular with Cork audiences.

Standards were being set by quality international adjudicators. Aloys Fleischmann was easily able to get them because of his position in the Music Department in UCC. Commissioned works were sought and presented and discussed at very influential seminars in UCC as part of the Festival.

As a teacher did you find the Festival inspiring?

I would see school choirs every Thursday and Friday. You'd see young choirs and their teachers and within a few years you'd begin to see them in the evening performances. You'd see the whole process of evolution going on under your very eyes. The callow, shy conductor would in a few years be taking his bow with the best of them. That's how the Choral Festival bedded itself into becoming part of our national culture.

A lot of choirs could only come because people volunteered to put them up. The Eastern European choirs had very little money. Choirs would have their uniforms of course. They were bigger in the early days. Now there is a move towards chamber choirs. From Varna in Bulgaria we had a choir of nearly 300 people on one occasion. You'd be hoping to get them placed while you still had something to say. They would walk onto the stage in a seemingly endless stream. Most of them were lodged by willing volunteers who were happy to welcome these visitors to their homes.

The Cork caravan company made its summer caravan supply available to accommodate visiting choristers. A lot of religious institutions that had dormitories put them at the disposal of visiting choirs. The army provided meals for the four days of the Festival. They were seconded to serve meals in the Grand Parade Hotel. Cork was busy during the Festival. Hotels were full. It was the people's Festival at every level. This was a tremendous way of constructing a festival at small expense, and with maximum civic effect.

Your other musical involvements included directing for the Cork Operatic Society.

My first production for the Cork Operatic Society was *A Country Girl* by Lionel Monckton in the Father Mathew Hall in 1952 or 3. It was a traditional Edwardian musical comedy. Shortly after that we did a revue called *Operantics* in the Father Mathew Hall and then lo and behold the Opera House burnt down. With the loss of the Opera House we found ourselves in trouble. Der Breen came to the help of the Operatic Society by offering a date on the Palace stage. Although the Palace had become a cinema, the old stage was still there, rather cramped and more suited to music hall with limited wing space. I had become taken up with the new American musicals and wondered if we might change fairly radically from the Edwardian English musicals in our repertory and do the new American musicals – like *Oklahoma*. When I was doing *A Country Girl* I found that as the plot went on, things did not hang together very consistently. An old operatic man, Jack Cronin, brought in a libretto of the original production in Daly's of London in 1904. It was twice as long as the one I was working with. I learnt that musical comedy altered in its form as there were cast changes, etc. It wasn't Shakespeare. There was no need to defend the librettist. It was a practical business. You cut and added as you wished or needed.

Dance was an essential component of these new musicals. For example there is a large ballet in the middle of *Oklahoma* in which the good and evil forces are played out. By contrast, dance in the Edwardian English musical comedies was demure and graceful and not very dramatic. We continued working in the Palace once a year and did *Annie Get Your Gun* in which David McInerney, one of our finest actor baritones, and Mary O'Donovan gave superb performances. Mary was a superb Annie and also played Moll in John B. Keane's *Moll*. We had a whole flock of Carlyles from the very musical Carlyle family. Bob Carlyle was a very good singer. We did *Finian's Rainbow*. It deals with the black problem in terms of Irish shamrockery. 'How are things in Glocca Morra' was a tune from it. The leading lady, Mary Cagney from Cork, gave a wonderful performance. Cherry Hutson, daughter of Marshal, the artist who taught at the Crawford School of Art for many years, stole the show with a poignant dance performance of the young deaf and dumb girl. We did a continental musical, *White Horse Inn*.

Joan Denise did the choreography and dancing for several of the productions. In working with the Cork Operatic Society for over twenty years I met a group of people who became my friends and collaborators, including people like Mon Murphy. Mon is one of the great Cork artists. Mon was very versatile and she kept up her contribution all along. I can recall her being harassed by a dance instructress early on in her career saying 'you can't do it dear, can you?' But Mon always captured audiences.

You and Der Breen were barely 30 years of age when the Film Festival got under way.

Yes, but the success of the festivals, the Film Festival especially, meant a loss to me. Der Breen had to give up work in the theatre as he became a full-time organiser. In a very short time the Film Festival absorbed an enormous amount of time in organisation and in travel, with the result that Der's years in PTG came to an end. The last ten years of PTG, before it became absorbed into Everyman in 1963, were run largely by me. He had been the main director for the first ten years of its life – it had begun in 1942 or 3 as part of a wider scheme of extra-curricular activities for the school and younger past pupils. Our three in a row – *Journey's End, The Black Stranger* and *Thunder Rock* – meant that PTG got a successful life of its own. These three plays were essentially directed by Der, and I played the leads. Anyone could see that Der dealt sympathetically with these three quite contrasting plays produced in the Father Mathew Hall over a period of a few years when he was still a very young man.

With the success of *An Tóstal*, Der's involvement in PTG came to an end. So I became director in PTG. I had started as an actor. I imagine I would have turned to directing, but later rather than sooner. People like Michael Twomey helped a great deal. He is younger than I am but acquired expertise and quickly matured as an actor to become the all-round, successful theatre man that he is. He helped to bridge the gap left by Der, first as an actor and subsequently as a director. I wasn't on my own.

One of the sad features of Der's absorption in the two great festivals, the Choral for a time and then the Film Festival, was that his lifestyle was adversely affected. He developed a serious alcohol problem, without the homely process of adjustment that most of us had. I didn't drink much, if at all, until I finished university. When I was earning a bit of money I enjoyed social drinking. He missed out on

Der, Vida and Dan.

that. He came from a family that had very strong views on temperance. I remember him wearing a pioneer pin. He came into drinking quite late, from the wrong angle and became a lone drinker under pressure. He wasn't in any way a lonely man. He was full of music and joy in his youth. One of the things Brother Jerome said was that he suffered from a profound depression. It was so tragic that Der's life became clouded by a late onset of depressive drinking. Der had a great warmth and a gift of grappling friends to himself with hoops of steel, as Shakespeare said. He never lost a friend. We all remained deeply friendly with him during his short life. If there was a problem during a Festival he had friends who would be there. Harry Conboy in City Hall was a man who, if there was a need, would act with utmost discretion and loyalty. Der did grapple strongly with the problem of alcohol. In his usual outgoing way he became a very outgoing member of Alcoholics Anonymous and tried to help others. Vida his wife stood by him through very difficult times but he died prematurely.

Her brother Jim Daly was a very active man in PTG and played one of the leading parts in *Journey's End*, before departing like so many others to earn his crust in Dublin. Vida's father was the CEO of the Vocational Educational Committee, a very nice man. Der became a film censor later on, in 1972 I think; a reward I suppose for all the work he had done for the Festival. He was in Dublin when he died suddenly.

The Film Festival's miracle days were in the Savoy, a place full of elegant spaciousness. It was a huge art deco film theatre which opened in 1932 and claimed the loyalty of Cork hearts for decades.[33] The Savoy Sunday nights were legendary. It's hard to say how many young lovers enjoyed the Savoy on a Sunday night. It accommodated an enormous crowd and had large spaces in front with a restaurant and foyer that made it perfect for a film festival. The Savoy was an Arthur Rank cinema, part of the Rank circuit. Rank was a huge entrepreneur who bought cinemas everywhere. He made films too, Rank Films, whose name led to a lot of puns. They were very co-operative with the Festival.

Der, as they say in *Casablanca*, gathered the usual suspects around him. Der's brother Kevin was a great worker in all the Film Festivals until his death. Bernard Curtis in the School of Music worked for the Festival and Moira Pine looked after difficult matters of guest protocol and all the public press side. You'd have ambassadors present and a stream of guests coming and going.

My role in the Festival was moderately extensive. Der had a strong view that no film, long or short, in a foreign language should go out without some kind of communication with the audience. He wanted to keep the Festival close to the Cork people. A night's programme might have three or four foreign shorts. You might have a seriously scientific film on a sometimes complex subject that would be unin-telligible without some kind of understanding. No way could you let a German film on new methods in steel manufacturing on the Ruhr, with perhaps a very serious script, loose on the unfortunate cinema-going public without help. Der always got a copy of the soundtrack which he would have translated. That was where my work really came in. He insisted I would do a live commentary. I would view the films beforehand. Then I would go into the projection box where the real heroes of the Festival worked. Derry and Dan in the Savoy worked around the clock. They made a little device with a switch so that I could come in over the soundtrack and read the English translation over the film as presented and cue it. If you had a funny soundtrack you might have to do a bit of live entertainment. That went on for eight or nine years. These foreign language films were shown to the juries beforehand in their strict original form. For the purists, what I did was not appreciated.

I was a presenter in the early years, both in the Savoy and the Capitol. I continued my own contribution in the Palace where Der was all-year-round manager, but when the Festival transferred to the Opera House I finished my connection with the Film Festival. Having presented so many of the opening and closing nights and discussions on stage of the Film Festival for over twenty years I can say that the effect of walking onto the Savoy stage and looking out at a vast auditorium with a great breadth of people and its vast height as you looked up to the gods and upper circle was absolutely extraor-dinary. At first it was quite a daunting business to open your mouth at all.

Was it very formal?

Der insisted on everyone, including guest speakers, wearing dress suits. Some abhorred wearing black tie. But I think it was a morale thing with Der and it made protocol easier. It was *de rigueur* for people going on to the Festival Club in City Hall also.

You must have had about ten dress suits.

I had three. My friend Joe Fitzgerald from Fitzgerald's menswear shop fixed me up. I had a little black notebook with my notes in it, which was invisible against the black suit.

Were you on many of the juries?

A tricky problem in the early Festivals was adapting to the needs of the censorship laws. All the films had to be viewed and juries drew up reports for them. We all served on those juries. The censorship people had to be happy that all films to be viewed were suitable. But they bent over backwards so that the Festival could be a kind of a club for the presentation of artistic films.

The actual programme of the Film Festival was a mixed bag. The official awards were all in the short film category because the international film body were trying to preclude the proliferation of festivals everywhere. Cork was very lucky to get in. The federation were very supportive but you had to watch your Ps and Qs. Cork wasn't like Cannes or Berlin.

Cork also used the Festival to present films that were being issued more or less on the commercial circuit. We had splendid films. There were always genuine people of real talent there to promote films, many being shown for the first time. Der had good relationships with the film companies in London and secured releases for Cork. It was vital also to present Irish-made films and give them maximum coverage. Some of the Irish films premiered at the Festival were very interesting. *Mise Éire* (1959) was the first full-length feature film made in the Irish language. Gael Linn produced and Louis Marcus was involved. That was very well received. One of Louis D'Alton's plays *This Other Eden* was an Ardmore adaption for the screen and premiered the same year.[34] While Der did not have as strong an interest in the Irish language as I had, he had a strong sense of national identity. He was from a Fianna

Front row l–r: Jack Lynch, Jack Cotter, Der Breen. Back: Dan Donovan.

Fáil background. It was very much part of his policy that any recently made Irish film or any Irish film in the offing should have a place in the Festival programme.

Der felt that as well as the awards for short films we should have our own best actor or actress award – purely local – not anything to do with the international film board – so we'd have our own little jury with prizes for key categories to give some recognition to matters of quality, to bring some of the commercial films into the frame of the Festival as it were. I acted on that jury for many years. I'd see pre-screenings. Jim Stack, the Neesons and Michael Twomey and a whole lot of my theatrical friends rallied round to form juries.

Did cinema and theatre overlap in your imagination?

They did. It was all part of the establishing of a national body of work, in whatever discipline, that would be in the national interest. That Corkery-ism never really left me.

Were you conscious that Sean O'Faolain was director of the Arts Council from 1956 to 1959?

No, I wasn't. I'm surprised to hear it. In those days it was still small, a gradually expanding bureaucracy. I think as our problems expanded later on they became more aware of the needs of groups like ours or the Yeats Summer School in Sligo; groups outside Dublin. I do know that Sean O'Faolain would have been supportive from the contact I had with him on a radio committee.

Tell me more about the presentations.

The whole idea was to get ordinary people to feel they were welcome, so nearly every night there would be a stage presentation with stars or directors or distinguished critics on stage. I remember Vittorio De Sica, leader of Italian post-war Realist cinema being there. Despite the vastness of the Savoy, these stage presentations were hugely looked forward to.

In addition to the special programmes of shorts, documentaries and commercial releases there were the tribute programmes. François Truffaut came for his own film *Les Quatre Cents Coups/The 400 Blows* (1959) and was invited to return for a tribute programme. I had the privilege of introducing him in the Capitol cinema over a week. When cinema began to get into trouble with the advent of television, support for the Savoy fell away. Gradually it reached the stage where the whole network and the Savoy, with its restaurant and foyer, got into financial trouble. When it closed, the Festival transferred to the Capitol on Grand Parade. The Ward Anderson Film Distribution Company had it. They survived longer and were very supportive too. Six or seven of Truffaut's major films were introduced in the Capitol. He presented each of them and attended each of the screenings. He was a bit sensitive about his English but it was very good. He was quiet spoken, charming and utterly co-operative and anxious to do what was required. The bigger they come, the nicer they are, I find.

I'll make an exception to that observation. Otto Preminger was the only director I found a little unpleasant. Jean Seberg gave her debut performance in his *St Joan*, based on Shaw's *St Joan*, adapted for screenplay by Graham Greene. Really Otto was heavy going. When we were discussing my introduction to the audience I made a slight slip-up. I said 'St Joan as in the saint.' I forgot to mention Shaw. 'No, No,' he said, 'it's Shaw's version'. I said 'Maybe it's important for the audience to know that'. 'Why don't you make the same mistake you made just now on stage and I will correct you?' he said. So we did that on stage. The film was a dud. It was sad for Jean Seberg. I don't think her career ever lived up to expectations. I think he was an overwhelming director, the wrong director for her. Instead of evoking a performance from her, he laid his heavy hand on the whole concept of the film.

Was it great fun having film-stars and directors around town?

In the early days people gathered in the streets to see all the distinguished guests arriving in their limos from the Metropole and the Imperial, people like Dawn Adams and her prince husband and people of her ilk. I think Ford provided the limos. Two or three would do the work, as the Metropole and the Imperial were close to the Savoy and City Hall and later the Capitol, the Palace and the new Opera House. The Film Festival is still successfully held annually in the Opera House and other cinemas. There were always a great number of starlets, girls being tutored for stardom. All the Rank starlets would be there and starlets from Italy and Germany. The film companies made sure that all opportunities for press coverage were taken. The girls would arrive escorted by members of the local committee, rather like the Roses in Tralee. The crowd would press forward as the limos arrived. The stars were handed out in their beautiful evening dresses. If the local escorts were accompanying a particularly beautiful diva, they'd get a gee-up from the crowd. Their blushes weren't spared. That peculiarly warm local thing was always there. There was a kind of pride that all these famous people were coming to Cork and here was Cork a centre for fashion and attraction. You'd have the odd burst of disappointment: 'Ah Jayus, it's only

Dicky Beamish,' or 'it's only Gus Healy'. It was only a local star. There'd be a fair bit of ball-hopping.

Once they entered the Savoy the stars moved through the palatial grandeur of the huge space. There were steps and balconies for pauses. It was a pretty tight journey backstage but that did not affect the splendid spectacle of the grand arrivals.

The story of Dawn Adams and the milk bath has come down in history. There's a classic apocryphal version that Bernard Curtis used to tell very well, in a dry, droll School of Music kind of way. Douglas Vance the manager of the Metropole, a wonderful hotelier, is the other character in the story. One of the minor flunkies comes to Mr Vance. 'Mr Vance, that actress Dawn Adams want a milk bath.' 'Of course if she wants a milk bath she can have one,' says Mr Vance. 'What will I do so, Sir?' 'Go out and get three crates of bottles of milk and pour the milk into the bath.' 'Right so, Mr Vance.' Off he goes and gets the three crates of milk and pours them into the bath. She enjoyed her bath, leaving the milk in the bath. 'Mr Vance, there's a full bath of milk there. What will I do with it?' asks the flunky. 'Don't waste it. Get the bottles and fill them,' says Mr Vance. Off he goes and bottles the milk. An hour or so later he comes back and says 'Mr Vance what am I going to do with the three or four pints left in the bath ...?' This was the Dawn Adams story embellished, localised and maybe vulgarised; the plain man's reaction to some of the more nonsensical things that happened in the Film Festival from time to time.

People gathered to see people arrive at the Festival Club in City Hall in the early days. People as I say were expected to wear black tie. The stage party would adjourn there, where there was food and drink and bands for dancing. I remember wandering over to City Hall one night just before the main crowd came over and finding James Mason having a quiet drink at the bar. He was a self-effacing man and seemed to be quietly avoiding the melee. I remember finding him very charming.

Policing City Hall was a very big job. Der had good relations with all the public officers and the guards were very helpful. The law was being bent all over the place. I recall Charles J. Haughey closing the Film Festival one Sunday night. The presentation of prizes for the winning competition in the short film category was done quite quickly. When he came over to City Hall after the closing ceremony, all the bars were closed. In those sanctified days you only got your bar extension on Sunday night from twelve o'clock when you entered Monday. You opened the bars when midnight struck. The bold Charlie came in with his entourage. He looked around and saw the shutters of the bar. The chief superintendent said 'Minister, we are waiting for twelve o'clock when we can officially open the bars for the extension.' Charlie looked around in that baleful way of his and said 'For Christ's sake open the f…ing bars'. I recall the sudden rush as the bar shutters moved. All rushed to the Valhalla of the bar. The Festival was indeed closed. It showed the pragmatic side of Charlie.

7

The Summer of Sive

You were creatively involved with the playwright John B. Keane[35] who was only two years younger than you and Seán Ó Tuama. How and when did all that begin?

So much was going on that I was completely unprepared for events that were to make a tremendous change in my own life and in Cork theatre. It happened quite accidentally. James N. Healy had a tremendous record in Cork theatre. As a schoolboy in Christians he acted in Gilbert and Sullivan. He showed precocious talent and a complete flair for every aspect of stage work. From early on he showed a propensity to become a star in music and acting. He was ten years older than me. When I was a child I saw one of the productions he was in at the Opera House, directed by John Daly. James N. became one of the leading members of the Cork Operatic Society, doing all kinds of musical comedy including Gilbert and Sullivan over many years. In 1950, he founded the Gilbert and Sullivan [G&S] Group with many of his friends and old associates. That remained one of the chief musical societies in Cork for many years.

From the whole gamut of work James N. did, I knew him. He was outstanding. He could read music and was a very skilful producer and director. I had worked with him because in PTG we were accustomed to putting on a Passion play at Easter in the Opera House and

121

on one occasion James N. joined his old school rivals and took the part of Judas. He was interested in straight acting as well as musicals. He also had various comic characters he would play – he did Ned the Gom and other characters which were broadcast.

He was an accountant and worked in Ford's, the great car manufacturers in Cork. Some time in the late 1950s he was head-hunted by another Cork firm, a well-known timber firm [Eustace's]. He had to do a great deal of heart-searching. Ford's were considered to be one of the best and most stable employers around. Once you got in you had a job for life. Loyalty to the firm was part of the Ford ethos and strength over the years. James N. felt very worried. He realised that if he left them there was no going back. At any rate he decided to take the timber firm's offer and within a year or two his new job petered out. One of his biggest tasks there was arranging for its liquidation. He was heading for unemployment at a rather bad time.

He consulted his friends and one of the options he felt he might have was becoming a professional in theatre. He was working in the Opera House and doing G&S and he was doing variety work. If he could get his act together there might be a full-time job. Most people who became professional left Cork. Jim's mother had died when he was only a few months old and he lived with three aunts in Lincoln Place at the top of Grattan Hill – in the house that Thackeray stayed in on his Irish visit. He had a tremendous loyalty to those three aunts. Auntie Ben was in poor health always. Another worked in the accountancy firm Bass & Co., they've now gone. Aunt Rose was the really important one. She cared for him and she worshipped him. She had been a member of the old Operatic Society and she was intensely loyal to him, going to all his performances. That was something I shared with him. We were brought up in a largely female house with aunts looking after us. Rather extraordinary.

He had to get into his professional theatre career very carefully. He came to me and said 'How about developing the legit drama?' That was what we called it, the legitimate drama, 'the legit'. Could he add that as a string to his bow as it were? I had seventeen years of theatrical experience behind me at that stage. I had been into the economics of it when I took up teaching. Jim Stack had too. Literally to do his theatre work he had to teach voice production. I gave an Irish drama class in the School of Music in the 1950s when Compántas Chorcaí was established and Jim was there, teaching English drama. Bernard Curtis, the head of the School of Music, was a very intelligent man and saw that these things had to be attended to. You could do it Jim Stack's way.

At the start I wasn't desperately encouraging, as I said, having been through the finances myself. Over 52 weeks of the year I reckoned it wouldn't be very good. But luckily then another friend of mine, Barry Hassett, a commercial traveller in insurance or cars, very involved in theatre, came to me. He had been travelling in Kerry. The talk of Kerry was a new play by a Kerry man, John B. Keane, a publican from Listowel. Barry saw it, in Killarney I think. He was very enthusiastic in his account of the play. He said we should get hold of it and put it on in Cork, it was theatre dynamite. It made a tremendous impression on Barry. It was powerful, richly coloured. Keane was a new voice in the theatre. This play was called *Sive* – it has since passed into history. James N. was dithering at the time. I rang him immediately and said I had just heard that there was a tremendous new play doing the rounds in Kerry, by a publican in Listowel, John B. Keane. If he could manage it he should get down to see it. If all that was said about it was even half true it could kickstart James N. into his professional career. He went down to Listowel and saw the production, which was magnificent. Listowel had quite a cultural kick to it. George Fitzmaurice, one of the great Abbey actors, was from there. And of course there was Bryan MacMahon.

The rather daunting president of UCC, Professor O'Rahilly, was from Listowel, wasn't he?

He was. Listowel was an interesting place. James N. went out to the pub, spoke to John B. – I think it was a brief conversation – and asked him could we do the play in Cork. John B. asked him a few sharp questions and said 'You can have it'. It is worth noting that the Abbey had succeeded in rejecting the play by then. That's how Cork got the first professional production of *Sive*.

I succeeded in seeing the play in the Killarney Festival. The PTG presented *The Queen and the Rebels* by Ugo Betti. It had won at the Cork Festival. The result at the Killarney Festival was: First Prize *Sive*, produced by the Listowel Group; Second Prize *The Queen and the Rebels*, produced by PTG. Jim Fitzgerald from the Gate was the adjudicator. As a sop he gave me a little silver cup for direction. Jim was great. A bit fond of the bottle, died young. The standards were very good in the 1950s, and rising. Jim was thrilled when we arrived in Killarney with our stage carpenter and our lighting man, moving in like the old travelling players.

The practical problems of producing *Sive* began. We invited some people up from Listowel. Sive, the girl, was played by Margaret Dillon and the wife was played by Norah Relihan. Pats Bocock, the tinker father, came up. Rehearsals began in the old Group Theatre in South Main Street. James N. rented the old Beamish Social Club and it became headquarters. It had a little theatre of 100 seats and the front room upstairs was a great rehearsal space. John B. was one of the best writers for any company doing his plays. He attended rehearsals regularly but not invariably. He was part of the general planning work, making suggestions, being available, rewriting.

I suppose he'd drive up to Cork fairly easily from Listowel?

Yes, Cork was the capital of Munster as it were. Mary his wife was a

Southern Theatre Group in Sive *in Father Mathew Hall, 1959. Nora Relihan and Kay Healy of the Listowel Players and James N. Healy.*

great support to him in running the pub and he had a good barman too so he had a lot of backing in getting time to write.

On 29 June 1959 the Southern Theatre Group presented *Sive* at the Father Mathew Hall, the first of 255 performances. James N. couldn't have got a better professional start. Molly Keane's play

Spring Meeting was being rehearsed that spring but the sensational success of *Sive* meant that the production of *Spring Meeting* went on hold and then wasn't done at all. James N. was very disappointed. He used to go to Ardmore, and was a personal friend of Molly Keane, who wrote under the name of M. J. Farrell. He was very anxious to do her play but she understood, and didn't mind. It was a light, amusing, social comedy and had been presented very successfully in London in the 1930s.

Sive ran for six weeks that summer. It was known amongst us as 'the summer of *Sive*'. I played Mike Glavin. It was a marvellous start for the Southern Theatre Group [STG], but there was no point in going on unless the company had inbuilt continuity. What followed was getting a company together. The formation of the Southern Theatre Group was on a very ad hoc basis. The company was formally established with three directors: James N. as company secretary and manager, Frank Sanquest, who was the scene designer at the Opera House and myself as chairman.

Sive wasn't just a phenomenon on its own. Immediately after it, we had some more of his country plays. Keane was catching a rich vein of rural life with its poverty and limitations and lack of infrastructure. It was a way of life that led to powerful frustration and powerful emotions, which John caught when it was on the point of disappearance. The plays held a mirror up to that way of life. The tensions and the loneliness in small isolated communities – he caught all these things. Hence powerful theatre. Part of that scenario in *Sive* would be the made match. There was a dark, bitter part in that the young girl was being married to the old man: 'For the ould man have the money for the child' was one of the lines. Keane was a master of the language and a great recorder of the voices and ballad lines he would have heard. He had a great sharpness in picking up that authentic detail with enormous vividness. Whatever the contrivance of the plot, there was a total authenticity to the people he knew. The Abbey were often accused of romanticising Irish country life; of idealising and disinfecting the 'PQ', as it was called, the peasant question.

Sive was a play that appealed enormously to women. John saw that the role of women could not continue as it still was in some parts of rural Ireland. There were three women in *Sive,* the bitter old grandmother, the frustrated ambitious daughter-in-law, not in a happy marriage to Mike Glavin and of course the catalyst, the young innocent Sive, who is to be manipulated and dragooned into marriage to an old man who has the money to give him social mobility. His name – Seán Dóta – has the sound of doting. James N. was very good in the character of the matchmaker, who brought home the contrast between them and drove home theatrically the dreadful fate that was ahead of girls like Sive. She was a victim. We see him viewing his matchmaking as his craft which has a social benefit. 'I know what a man have to do who have no woman to lie with him' he says, speaking of personal frustration. You then begin to see the thing from the point of view of Seán Dóta – this gives resonance to the part of the matchmaker.

In STG we would do a longish summer season and go again in March, with touring in between. Life was moderately busy during the year. James N. had a number of people who were available, but not all the time. Kay Healy – who was now widowed, a Listowel woman who lived in Cork – and others were always available from Listowel. Kay played right through as the grandmother in *Sive* and helped in many ways, organising the passengers of tour buses to visit performances. After the Cork success with *Sive,* we immediately had requests for touring. Tours that were very far away presented problems. I was restricted to holidays from school. Requests had to be managed very carefully. It was often necessary for me to drive to nearer places, like Limerick and back again. You'd have to drive three or four of the other players. You were out late at night, coming back to face work the following morning. STG was run on a shoestring and cut right across my life in terms of the unexpected demands on time and energy that it made.

Michael McAuliffe as Liam Scuab in Sive.

Did you take many Keane plays to Dublin?

John B.'s early plays were divided between STG and Phyllis Ryan of Gemini Productions in Dublin. She had done one of John B.'s first urban plays – she did many productions of his for the first time. We shared premieres with Gemini and John B. could please himself as to who would play certain plays best.

On one of the early Dublin trips we were greatly welcomed by Stanley Illsley and Leo McCabe, who managed the Olympia. Stanley Illsley, who formed the well-known Illsley–McCabe Company in the Olympia, first came to Cork as a member of the Clopet–Yorke company. While on holidays, Betty visited Erdigg, the mansion[36] of Yorke, a very cultivated Welshman from the minor aristocracy. Clopet of course carefully chose an excellent company, many of whom returned to Cork year after year and played a long summer season in the Opera House, the CYMS and the Father Mathew Hall. Stanley and Leo had heard on the bush telegraph about *Sive*. We were always encouraged by the Cork caucus in Dublin. Jack Lynch, when minister and later Taoiseach, and Máirín his wife, never missed a production of ours at the Olympia. He was proud of our visits there and he and Máirín always came backstage to meet and greet the cast, which was more than you could say for many of the Dublin professionals who bitterly resented our being in Dublin, even though the Abbey had originally rejected *Sive*.

Apart from setting up the production, which meant a weekend in Dublin, there was some row over allowances for staying in Dublin. We had been handed a box office hit but had no real organisation. We had to allow for digs money. It fell to James N. to make arrangements. Eventually, there was a bit of a disagreement. Lots of people were involved, including Equity, the actors' union. The result was that we had to structure the company legally. When the Dublin production of *Sive* was over, a number of people left or weren't re-employed. We replaced them with great difficulty and learnt a very sharp lesson about venturing into territory where we weren't competent to deal with all the snags.

We generally stayed in cheaper hotels and maybe occasionally in good B&Bs. Where possible we would be together but we would always be in the same area. The expense allowances weren't great but we saw a lot of Dublin life. I remember being in Rathmines and travelling in by bus. I remember another time lodging near the Olympia itself. The Olympia had been a Dan Lowrey[37] music hall, just like the Palace.

I remember one woman in particular. She had a fine old house not far from the Gaiety. She was a lovely woman, married to a garda sergeant. Most of us were booked in there for one particular production. It might have been a Keane play, *Rain at the End of Summer* (1967). I remember Tom Vesey, one of our character actors trained by Fr O'Flynn, was there. Tom had a very good face and great authenticity. He got a new lease of life with STG. Another one of our members, Donal O'Donovan, used to give Vesey a hard time over his long period in the Loft with Fr O'Flynn, whom he idolised. Donal grew a little weary of hearing the praises of the priest being sung. He used occasionally break out and yell at poor old Tom in a sort of comic way not to be bothering him about the priest. Not that that stopped Tom. In sheer frustration – Donal was kind of pent up – someone said to him 'Take it easy, this is a garda's house'. Donal went over and threw up the window and shouted onto the street 'F… the guards'. We had visions of spending the night in a cell.

There was that tedium of hanging around, waiting for someone else, a phone call, a publicity shot. You were always at someone else's beck and call. As I was so often directing and also playing cameo parts, I'd have both sides of the experience. James N. had a grandiose thing, he'd love us all to be around when it would be nicer for us to be able to head off to Howth or somewhere. He had a proprietary interest in the company as his people. That would ease off as the week ran and the publicity was done. I spent a good deal of pleasant times on the beaches of Howth and Killiney. Peculiarly enough, you wouldn't see what was on in Dublin theatre, as you'd be playing yourself. Even getting to a matinee often required coming up on a separate occasion.

Was there great excitement wondering what play John B. might turn up with next?

One thing seemed to follow another. Next thing we had a splendid play, *Sharon's Grave*, which the Abbey rejected also. It had another marvellous thing like the tinker in *Sive*. Dinzie on his pony! His pony was the man who carried him around on his back. Flor Dullea, one of our regulars, a huge man, played the pony. Flor was a national school teacher. We had a lot of teachers because they could play during the holidays. Eamonn Keane, John's brother, played Dinzie for us at John's behest. He only acted with us once. He was a memorable Dinzie, a fine actor but a bad alcoholic. He came from London to our first rehearsal in Cork. We were rehearsing in the Group Theatre and heard he'd arrived in Cork earlier in the day. But there was no sign of him. We sent members of the company out to hotels and guest houses to see was there any news. Eventually a taxi driver called at the door. The taxi driver had been looking for the rehearsal room. Our first introduction to the bold Eamonn was when he was carried into the rehearsal by the taxi man. Luckily we had perfect casting for that occasion. I'd got a magnificent pony for him, the *grámhar* Flor Dullea. Eamonn was a ringer for the part of Dinzie, small, wizened, beady eyed. It was visually a delight. Eamonn was splendid. There is a superb love scene with Trassie and the thatcher Peadar Minogue, played by Séamus Moynihan. Dinzie the cripple is a twist on the frustration theme. John didn't shirk from depicting the mental disorder springing from frustration. Dinzie is the crippled man who desired and who had to travel on another man's back. In the most leering way, he assumed he would marry Trassie.

The frustrations in society then led to a certain amount of disorder. I suppose after the Famine too there could have been inbreeding. The best stock went away maybe. I remember in Ballincollig, there was a square called the Mad Square. It was called that after the condition of some of the people living there. There was a woman called Katie who came out of her house with a poker in her hand one day and crossed over to the landlord's house, tapped the window with it, breaking the glass and then went back to her own house across the Square. I remember another woman who had a mildly deranged son and she kept him always upstairs, in the bedroom.

The asylum was the great dump, especially where land was involved. People mightn't be too bad but they were signed in, especially where there was land involved for their relations.

Eamonn Keane met Maura Hassett during that production of *Sharon's Grave*. The romance flourished during the rehearsals. Maura was a superb actress. She played Trassie. Maura was a neighbour of mine, from Doyle Road. She was behind me in College and was very active in Dramat. She was Barry Hassett's sister, very bright, very pretty, very talented, already making a big reputation on the pro-am stage in Cork. Eamonn had the gift of the gab. He had a romantic turn of speech. They fell in love and were married in Ballyphehane early in 1960. We had bannerettes with the masks of Tragedy and Comedy to greet them outside the church but the priest objected to these pagan symbols. Eamonn and Maura later went to Dublin. I was put out because one of the company's best actresses was taken from us. Maura eventually went back to teaching when the marriage failed.

What else of human interest can you remember in those early Keane productions?

Michael Twomey, a fine actor, played the tinker's son in *Sive*. The son was a simpleton, a *duine le Dia*. Then in *Sharon's Grave* he played Neelus who was also a bit of a gom, a simpleton, and in the next play we did, done originally by Gemini, *The Highest House on the Mountain,* he played Sonny. 'Dan, are you trying to give me a message? You've cast me in three plays as a fool,' asked Michael. Michael had impeccable instinct for a part, great discretion and control. He was and is a stalwart. I remember on one occasion in *Sharon's Grave* Eamonn came over to Michael and caught him by the hand and crushed a fresh rather than a hard-boiled egg into his hand, instead of the watch. Michael continued acting without batting an eyelid.

There was another occasion involving the stage manager, Charlie Ginnane, Eamonn and me. You were never without a job and I was 'on the curtain', as we say, one particular night. The rule is if you are caught onstage, run with the curtain, and dash into the wings. I pulled the curtain for the interval and after the interval checked to see that the stage manager was offstage. I couldn't see properly. I opened the curtain to discover the stage manager still on stage. The other side of that was that he was playing the corpse in *Sharon's Grave* and was still wearing the habit. So I opened the curtain to the audience with the corpse walking on the stage. He should have dashed for the wings, but he dashed for the door of the set, half pulling it down. Eamonn had an entry shortly and sized up the situation. He had great presence of mind. 'He-he Neelus' he improvised, 'Up to your tricks again' and put the door back on its hinges. They passed it off.

Another night there was nearly a row on the road coming back from Dungarvan after a performance there. I was driving as usual. Flor said 'My God, Maura is a great professional.' Eamonn took offence at Flor's respectful comments on his wife's superb acting. We got out of the car, presumably to relieve ourselves, and I said 'For God's sake, stop this rubbish.' But it simmered away on the road the whole way back to Cork.

Tell me more about working with John B.

He could cut and rewrite extensively. As regards cutting, a play in which I had a very big part to play was *The Crazy Wall* (1974*)*. The leading man was a schoolmaster, perhaps loosely based on John's father, who was a schoolmaster. It was written for me, which created problems with James N. who largely did the leads. I also had to direct this play. Physically and mentally it was a most demanding play. It made serious demands on one's stamina. It was one of John's town plays. The theme was the schoolmaster who had a hobby, or even an obsession with, building a wall. His cronies in the Local Defence Forces, the LDF, came into it as good, satirical, comic relief.

In the last act however there was a scene between the husband and wife, a strong family scene where she takes up the cudgels against the crazy wall, the LDF and other things in an effort at reform. As often in John's plays the first two acts were splendid. The third I felt was too long. The first two act rehearsals went quite well. But the last act presented considerable problems. Maybe it was too close to the bone. John was writing around it and not confronting it. Certain things were overwritten, others not treated at all.

John would often sit at the rehearsals and cut with us. His scripts often contained a line which would explicate a point of character or a part of the plot that needed explication. Key rehearsals early on often had a workshop quality.

Máirín Morrish – another teacher – was playing the mother and I was playing the father. We rehearsed it as fully as possible and he agreed we'd try it out on the floor. Both of us gave him the best idea of how it would play. John calmly said 'I see. I know what's wrong.

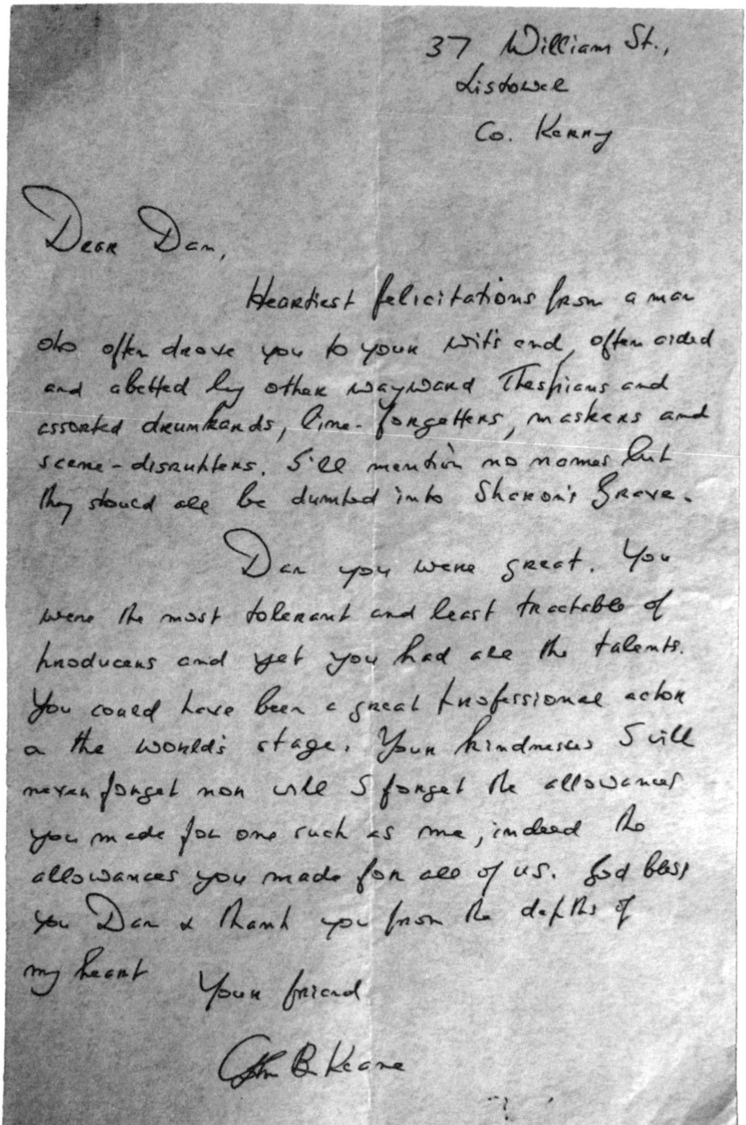

37 William St.,
Listowel
Co. Kerry

Dear Dan,

Heartiest felicitations from a man who often drove you to your wits end, often aided and abetted by other wayward Thespians and assorted drunkards, time-forgetters, maskers and scene-disrupters. I'll mention no names but they should all be dumped into Sharon's Grove.

Dan you were great. You were the most tolerant and least tractable of producers and yet you had all the talents. You could have been a great professional actor on the world's stage. Your kindnesses I will never forget nor will I forget the allowances you made for one such as me, indeed the allowances you made for all of us. God bless you Dan & thank you from the depths of my heart

Your friend

John B. Keane

A letter from John B. Keane to Dan Donovan c. 1992.

I'm talking around it, it requires cutting.' There and then he sat down and cut three pages. 'Let's kill these pages, they're not moving it on at all,' he said. He made further cuts, replacing them with crisp links that neatly dovetailed the cuts into the existing script. There were no rough cuts. It could play well. *The Crazy Wall* opened in the Municipal Theatre in Waterford to great success. We came back to Cork with it. It was to go to Dublin but I couldn't do the date agreed to play in the Olympia. I had to wait till the holidays came round. There was a little tension between me and John about that. There must have been frustrating aspects of dealing with us. James N. decided to play the part of the father. Reluctantly I had to agree. It was a bad move on James N.'s part. Our plays always did well in the Olympia and I suspect James N. wanted to keep up his tradition of playing the leads. I knew it wasn't quite James N.'s part. John wrote it for me. I gave James N. as much help as I could. There was a scene where the crazy wall has to come down and he takes a sledgehammer to it. There was no way of cheating on that. I found it enormously demanding physically. James N. didn't have the physical or mental stamina for that part. So it opened to poor notices. The success it had in Cork and Waterford wasn't forthcoming. John would have felt justice wasn't done to the play. It was one of the few occasions when I was seriously unhappy with what went out in my name, as I'd cast James N. in a hundred parts but not that one.

To indicate James N.'s strengths which developed enormously, and which touched on the personal thing, I remember him in the lead part in *The Year of the Hiker* (1963), one of John's most delicate plays, I think. Again, it picks up on a theme hinted at earlier, the ne'er-do-well husband who left and who returns, suffering from cancer, to die at home. James N. gave one of his finest performances in that role. It was the kind of thing I couldn't do in a fit. He dredged deeply into his own family history. There was trouble with his own father. He

James N. Healy and Dan Donovan in a Father Mathew Hall dressing room c. 1975.

confronted the domestic situation and used that to give depth and intensity to the dilemma of the Hiker coming back and the dilemma of the family and how to deal with it. The part was memorable. There was a good deal of searching which made the Hiker more sympathetic to the audience. It is a tender and quiet play. Our regular team, Michael Twomey, Ber Power, Flor Dullea, Kay Healy, Máirín Morrish and Loreta MacNamara were at their best.

The Year of the Hiker was a memorably good broadcast play. It was recorded and broadcast by us from Dublin.

Even when I stopped directing with Theatre of the South, in the late 1970s, James N., Jim as we all called him, was still mad to do it again. 'Look at the casting' I said 'You'd be all right as the father coming home with cancer, but you'd have to recast all the young people'. I had increasing problems with revivals.

Did you often do revivals?

Many Young Men of Twenty is a Keane play full of sadness, humorously caught, a play about emigration. We played it again and again. I thought I'd never get out of it. I played the pub owner. We had huge success with it. In the 1980s it was relevant again, it renewed itself.

On one occasion Siobhán O'Brien, a teacher from Cork, was playing Peg. Keane had written the part for her. She had to sing a sentimental song about her love affair which left her with an illegitimate baby. She was in the middle of John's melody when a lady we knew who was in her cups and sitting in the dress circle stood up and said 'Never mind that old thing, Siobhán, give us *Under the Bridges of Paris*'. Siobhán was a very talented singer and had a very good line in Edith Piaf.

Near the start of the play, I have a chat with Siobhán. In one particular

Southern Theatre Group production of Many Young Men of Twenty. *l–r: Flor Dullea, Siobhán O'Brien, Dan Donovan.*

performance when James N. was due on, Siobhán and I had finished our dialogue. No sign of James N. Very rare with him. Here we were, missing our leading man. I was notorious for inventing dialogue. She was knitting in the snug, waiting for the crowd to gather for the train. 'What's that you're knitting there, girl?' I ask. The play had been going on for quite some time and the garment had assumed rather voluminous proportions. 'That's just a little thing for the child' she said. 'You'd want to be careful, girl' I said 'or he could get lost in it'. Then we heard the patter of feet and James N. arrived, rather flustered.

John B. had been an emigrant to England himself and so was still writing as an insider.

He was. There was another side to the going away: those who went away didn't always do well. John caught that in *Hut 42* (1962), a play premiered, oddly enough, in the Abbey as John's Abbey debut. John dealt with the navvies in England, the Irish fellows who went over and often did not return. We did it one summer and it went quite well. There is a lovely part of an old guy, the lonely exile, a tender and touching part beautifully played by Chris Sheehan. These fellows had a very lonely life, maybe sending a bit home. They were a sort of by-product of Irish life.

Did John write many parts with actors in mind?

James N. always claimed the part of The Bull McCabe in *The Field* (1966) was written for him. He was invited to the opening of the film and was heard to say that.

Do you like the film?

I think it's a horrible distortion of the play. It made the ending very melodramatic. *The Field* was one of John's greatest successes. Of course Ray McAnally made a tremendous impression in that part in the first production, which was in Dublin. The Dublin production was excellent. Eamonn Keane played the Bird. Ray was dead before the film was made, I think.

Would it have been put on in Dublin because Cork was too close to the tragedy on which it was based, the recent murder of Moss Moore?

I'm not sure. As John's fame was growing he gradually gave the revivals and some of the new plays to Dublin, to the Olympia or the Gaiety. All through, Phyllis Ryan and Barry Cassin in Gemini produced quite a lot of the plays.

I knew the area where the murder took place because I used to go to Kerry on holidays. The case was very widely talked about, but with some degree of reticence. It was like the *'Cá bhfuil sé?'* case in Waterford, the 'Where is he?' case of the missing postman. The tragedy of neighbours falling out over land and rights of way belonged to the warp and woof of people's lives. The rows were always known locally and not much talked about, which is one of the reasons they festered. They remained subliminal. With pressures like that on something so crucial as land, you'd never know when the pent-up force would erupt, all the more so in family disputes. You could go to no part of the country without coming upon serious or lingering disputes about land. As a country man John would have heard discussions about the ramifications of the Moss Moore case in the bar. Referring to the Waterford case as the *'Cá bhfuil sé?'* case is part of rural reticence. It's almost a way of not making it too open to outsiders.

John B. was a fluent Irish speaker?

He was a fluent Irish speaker but he was against making Irish compulsory. He was part of a group who were against the privileges that went with the learning and speaking of Irish – the extra marks in the exams and that kind of thing. He felt it was undemocratic. It created a coterie of first-class citizens. He would be very different from Seán Ó Tuama there. Daniel Corkery, like Seán, would have strongly supported Fianna Fáil as the party most likely to preserve the essentials of his powerful, early, nationalist vision.

John was very fertile at the time of *The Field*. There were two plays available. He was a many-sided writer. He wrote a musical called *The Roses of Tralee*. It was a mild satire on the Rose of Tralee festival. John was able to turn his hand to music – he had a flair for verse and song. James N.'s connections with musical theatre made this ballad musical successful. I looked after the play part and James N. did the musical side. It demanded considerable resources as it had a cast of hundreds. As it happened, John kept us all happy, but the fish had got away, the prime part of The Bull in *The Field*.

So did you not produce The Field*?*

Afterwards we did two productions of it, so James N. did do the part. It was interesting to see the difference. James N. had a delicate, sly cunning to his interpretation. The Bull had a powerful son who did the violence for him. James N. didn't have the might and physical presence. He would build himself up a bit but the violence was done through the son. The father did the blackmailing. There was a slightly different slant in the interpretation.

Did you do a fair variety of plays in STG and indeed Theatre of the South?

It would be a great mistake to think of STG or Theatre of the South as playing John B. Keane exclusively. Wherever possible we did new plays, with an emphasis on work by Munster playwrights. Among the most successful was Gerry Gallivan's play about Michael Collins, *The Stepping Stone*. It is hard in these days of change to think of how controversial and charged the atmosphere was when we decided to do this new play in 1963. The Civil War experience and heritage had not died away. There was quite a deal of tension before the opening. We had a bomb threat. The tense atmosphere of the first night when many prominent figures of the Rising and the Treaty attended was memorable. Many had not spoken since the days of their earlier political division. It was a kind of a cathartic thing. People dredged their memories of the old situations. There were conversations among sons and daughters of those being enacted on the stage. James N. was playing Cathal Brugha and a touching thing I remember was an old man in the bar afterwards calling him Charlie, not making the distinction between the acted part and Charlie Burgess, as Cathal Brugha was called.

Were things beginning to be strained in the company towards the late 1960s?

The company revolt in Dublin during the first production of *Sive* in the Olympia was perhaps due to the fact that the thing had taken off without the proper company structure. Perhaps there were inherent problems in the way the whole Southern Theatre thing took off to a degree none of us was prepared for. It required a fair deal of pragmatism to keep it together as long as we did. In time, the same tensions began to manifest themselves among two directors. I was friendly with both. There was a bit of a temperamental problem between James N. and Frank Sanquest. Board meetings became rows between James N. and Frank, with me looking like piggy in the middle. At most board meetings there would be a certain amount of bickering. There was a particularly bad occasion in the late 1960s and things were said which should not have been said. It broke into a serious argument. James N. threatened that he wouldn't put up with certain things that were said, said in anger, in fairness. We went our separate ways in 1971.

James N. went to Clonmel to direct a musical. He rang me, warning me to make no decision of any kind. He felt the dispute was going to have further consequences. I remained friendly with Frank. Frank could be an excellent scene painter and had done a magnificent set for me in an *Oklahoma* in the 1950s when I was directing for the Cork Operatic Society. We revived it for the new Opera House and I did not act. With some degree of reluctance I gave up the part of Jud Fry, which was excellently played by Siobhán O'Brien's husband Jack Riordan.

James N. said he couldn't give up his work in STG; it was his livelihood. He proposed to continue in whatever way he could legally manage. He decided STG should go into liquidation. He would start a new company with a cognate name. Theatre of the South was established with both James N. and me and the actor and director we were friendly with, Michael Twomey, as company secretary. We had all worked very well with Michael down the years, perhaps mainly on modern plays. Michael had experience in the Loft. I played Claudius in a *Hamlet* he directed for the Opera House and Marie Twomey played Gertrude.

For a James N. production of *The Merry Widow* a professional singer, Joyce Blackham, was booked. I think she was with Sadler's Wells. Professional singers seem to be even more prone than amateurs to suffering from throat problems. As she was singing the lead part of Anna it was looking as though the performance would have to be cancelled. James N. was at his wit's end until he remembered that there was a very good local soprano, Marie Twomey, wife of Michael, who knew the part and had done it previously. He decided if she were game and willing to prevent a disaster and costly cancellation he would ask her to undertake the long and demanding lead role, literally at a day's notice. Marie was a lovely actress and singer and of course very beautiful. After a little thought she said she'd have a go.

Michael and Marie Twomey.

Marie had a great temperament. She undertook the task and brought the house down. She had a triumph. Joyce fortunately recovered her voice and was able to perform for the end of the run. Jim's brainwave and Marie's performance combined to make one of the great Cork rescue acts.

With Michael on board as company secretary, the re-organisation of STG into the Theatre of the South meant that we now required a set designer. We had all worked on different stages already with the rising young designer Pat Murray who had real flair. We invited Pat to become a director. He preferred not to go on the board but became the scene designer.

Pat, like yourself and James N., lost a parent early in life. I've heard his mother was maid, wife and widow in the one year?

Yes. When I met Pat first he was a young carer. He was minding his mother and aunt. He was very sweet-natured as well as tough, a very nice combination. I came to be in a not dissimilar situation minding my two aunts and then my two sisters. They call it payback time, a payback I was delighted to do. I had to attend to those who had attended to me when I was orphaned at the age of fourteen. My aunt Lell died in 1964 and Kit in the early 1970s. Lell was 86 and Kit was 85.

Pat took his vocation very seriously indeed. After he finished in the Crawford [Municipal] School of Art he went on a study period to Bayreuth, where really he worked at the highest level with people of the highest quality. He worked with and knew Friedland Wagner. He introduced me to her when she came to Cork. She was charming and very gracious to everyone. She couldn't be

Friedland Wagner and Patrick Murray, 1966.

more affable. She was extremely cultivated and extremely sharp – it wasn't always light and love in the Wagner family. She was feted by Pat who was thrilled to show off this living part of his CV. Pat's great hotel was the old Imperial in the days when Leo Downes was manager there. They would also have ended up in the Oyster Tavern off Patrick Street no doubt.

Pat forged very strong links with Joan Denise Moriarty. These lasted until her death in 1992. They did a major ballet every year and Pat designed the sets. All his sets were meticulously researched. He also did the sets for Jim Stack. All in all, he became very much in demand, not only in Cork but he got commissions from Wexford and the DGOS and outside Ireland. The world was his oyster but he elected to base himself in Cork because of his mother and aunt. We were very lucky then in Theatre of the South that we were able to get a lien on his services. He became in effect part of Theatre of the South.

I became particularly conscious of Pat's work ethic during the three-week period between 25 June and 12 July 1972 when Theatre of the South were invited to San Francisco.

The O'Growney branch of the Gaelic League invited us over. O'Growney had written an Irish grammar for students in the early days of the Irish revival and they called their branch after him. San Francisco was full of ethnic groups who had a strong tradition of keeping cultural links with their countries of origins. There was strong rivalry among the groups. The O'Growney branch decided to get someone over from Ireland and somehow they got ourselves. We all had to work very hard to put on three plays, with a core group of between ten and twelve of us. I was directing *Sive* and *The Year of the Hiker* and playing Mike Glavin in *Sive*. The other play was *The Country Boy* by John Murphy from Mayo, who was working in Paramount Studios at the time. He came up from Los Angeles and

Theatre of the South company arriving in San Francisco. l–r: Patrick Murray, Dan Donovan, Mary Foley, Donal O'Donovan, Mrs Ann Quilter, Bernard McHugh, James N. Healy, Harry Gogarty, Mary Walsh, Lou Mullen, Kay Healy, Frank Duggan, Dick Healy, Michael Twomey, Máirín Morrish.

invited us down there for a night. He showed us around the studios. *The Country Boy* was an enormous success. It was full of comedy and sadness and the whole schizophrenia of the exile's return. It touched the nexus of emotions of a returning Yank trying to deal with a new Ireland. James N. directed it. It was a splendid play, with the caveat that it was a play that became dated within its own canon. John Murphy was a one-play man and it was the only great success he achieved.

As well as the three plays, James N. inevitably did a one-man show. It was called *Himself* and it was a personal piece with ballads and stories. Frank Duggan of Cha and Mia fame was his accompanist. Michael Twomey played the Fool in *Sive* and the son in *Year of the Hiker*. James N. was the matchmaker in *Sive* and the Hiker in *The Year of the Hiker*. Mary Walsh from Cork was Sive. Máirín Morrish was Mena Glavin in *Sive* and Freda in *The Year of the Hiker*. Flor Dullea and Kay Healy were in both the *Year of the Hiker* and *The Country Boy* while our regular stage manager Dick Healy, a cousin

Opening of the new Opera House in Cork, 31 October 1965. l–r: Cmdr Crosbie, Jack Lynch, President de Valera, Lord Mayor Desmond.

of Jim's, did his usual hard-working stint. We were renewing things we'd done together and putting them into a structure. But because we couldn't take sets with us, Pat had to improvise for all the sets. He had to work the hardest. They were all rather solid productions requiring realistic Irish settings. You couldn't cheat with black drapes. They were rooted plays. Pat had to find the clutter for them. I came to admire his imagination as well as his work ethic. We had a busy but vastly enjoyable visit, rehearsed in the mornings and enjoyed the mist that comes in from the Pacific Ocean in the afternoons. There were lovely trips across the bay to Sausalito. We encountered a great deal of Irish American culture. We went to meetings with the O'Growney group; I remember I had to give a lecture on Irish theatre. We were cultural ambassadors for our country, in effect. I worked with Pat on many other occasions but that one stays in my mind.

Some years before we went to San Francisco, I had done a production by the Cork Operatic Society for the re-opening of the Opera House. It was *South Pacific*. Pat designed the sets. The opening night of *South Pacific* was a nightmare. The lights went. Tony Moffat yelled out a number to the orchestra and they improvised in the dark until the lights came on. Many of them were members of the old Opera House orchestra and were familiar with the repertoire of musical comedy. They all knew one another and they gave us a recital until the lights came on.

The night the Opera House re-opened must have been a very emotional night.

Our exile in the Palace and the Father Mathew Hall for major productions came to an end with the completion of the new Opera House in 1965. There was a big celebration concert in which all those people and groups associated with work in the old building were asked to contribute to a great Gala performance on 31 October. There was a great turnout. All the distinguished people were there. It was a night of great nostalgia and great joy. Bill Twomey the manager was delighted, having been head and tail of all the fund-raising with all the committees, to see the Opera House open again.

The new Opera House lit up, 31 October 1965.

I suppose you had been involved in the fund-raising yourself?

Everyone was delighted that the long period of fund-raising was over. We had all been intensely involved. We went door to door fund-raising. Of course I felt proud about the fact that the Cork Operatic Society for whom I was directing had opened the fund-raising with *Oklahoma* in 1957. We had the afternoon matinee, the usual mid-evening show and a special midnight matinee to fund-raise one weekend. We were wrecked but elated by the result. I did my usual marathon; I directed and I played Jud Fry in the lovely old Palace Theatre then managed as a cinema by Der Breen.

For the opening Gala concert in the Opera House, Southern Theatre Group presented the tinkers' scene from *Sive* with Tom Vesey and Michael Twomey playing the two leads. The size of the stage was demanding enough. Inevitably we had a slight hitch. A young actor who was to play the tinker's son failed to appear for the dress rehearsal during the afternoon, to my considerable embarrassment, especially as Jim Stack was directing. I had to go and get Michael Twomey to replace the young actor and to make a return as the tinker's son. A somewhat disconcerted young man in full costume and rather the worse for the wear wandered into the old Group Theatre – christened 'Healy's Hall' after James N. by Donal O'Donovan – where we were rehearsing. He was horrified that he was not going on in the opening night of the new Opera House. The Cork Ballet Company and Joan Denise Moriarty presented a scene and really everyone who was anyone in Cork theatre including returned exiles were there. Micheál Mac Liammóir did a scene from *I Must Be Talking to My Friends* with his black wig slightly askew. It was the wig he normally used to perpetuate his adolescence.

I think we were all overwhelmed by the sheer size of the stage and felt something crucial had been lost in the new building, which did not have the warmth and intimacy of the old building. Pat Murray was one of the heroes of the night. With a little bit of imagination he set the entire medley of events effectively and simply and made everyone pretty confident. He was to play a very dominant role in the new Opera House which, because of the size of the stage, was challenging in itself.

Pat always would work very closely with the company that was producing, reading scripts and was always full of good humour. I remember doing Cole Porter's *Kiss Me Kate*, my last musical production in the new Opera House, in 1972. Pat came up with all the answers to the challenges with the set. He had a sense of tact and practicality as well as a lot of flair. He would never put you out on a limb with big expenses that might put you out of business.

The phenomenon of the prophet never recognised in his own country applied to Pat. He was insufficiently appreciated, not by those of us who worked with him, who knew and loved him and found him a great collaborator, but by the powers that be, as it were. I don't think the wider cultural community realised what a treasure we had. He worked modestly yet ambitiously to stage magnificent show after magnificent show for nearly 50 years. He never got recognition for the fact that he had dominated theatre design in Cork, for nearly every kind of group, for several decades.

He felt very bitter at the failure of the powers that be when he presented a very ambitious but workable proposal for 2005, Cork's year as European Capital of Culture. He planned a very elaborate exhibition of sets, models and costumes, programmes and posters to run in City Hall for two weeks. That would literally be a history of Cork theatre over the years and the many people who had been involved in theatre at so many levels could have enjoyed it. As far as I know, he had planned it in some detail and either never got a proper reply to his proposal or got a curt one much later.

8

Early Everyman Days

Film and television gradually encroached on theatre but not before Everyman Theatre took off in 1963.

When John O'Shea and I began to form Everyman, it was at a time when I was particularly interested in making sure that various theatrical efforts did not defeat their purposes and intentions, by mounting productions that would clash. John was particularly active in the organisation of this and brought his fresh mind and his organisational and argumentative skills to bear on bringing the new organisation into being. I was anxious also to keep on the tradition of work that I had started and maintained with PTG. I was actively involved through many parts of the year with the commercial work of STG and I wanted a vehicle to carry that very deep interest of mine – which I had developed after the War – in wider theatre, including American and European drama, if necessary subsuming the PTG into a new organisation. From the time that I achieved independent means, a summer rarely passed without a visit to London or Stratford and there I came across so many plays that had a Continental and American provenance. This encouraged me to attempt many of the plays that I enjoyed. Hence, for example, *The Country Girl* by Clifford Odets. I saw Michael Redgrave playing in it in the old St James's Theatre, which was knocked down or ceased to be a theatre some seasons later. He was a great favourite of mine. That brewed away in my subconscious and was the play that opened our first Everyman season in 1963. I adored Arthur Miller and Tennessee Williams and had ambitions to do plays, which we did eventually tackle, like *Cat on a Hot Tin Roof, Death of a Salesman* and *All My Sons*.

I'm sure you've heard the apocryphal story of Arthur Miller's visit to the Crawford Municipal Gallery, as it then was? Curator Der Donovan, conscious of the eminence of his visitor, went upstairs to tell the CEO and ask him to welcome the playwright there. 'Who is Arthur Miller?' asked the CEO, bothered at being interrupted from his VEC work. 'He's a writer, married to Marilyn Monroe' said Der. So down goes the CEO and says 'Welcome to the Crawford Gallery, Mr Monroe'.

You know Der Donovan, Díarmuid Ó Donobháin, was a great character and a lovely actor, playing many roles in Jim Stack's company. Another person from the Crawford who was involved with Jim Stack was Fred Archer, the silversmith. Fred made the Graduates Club medal for Student of the Year which I obtained in UCC. He and other members of the Archer family were loyal members of the company. Fred was very active in all the backstage activities. His wife was very involved as an actress. The loyalty of the Archers was a great thing for Jim. Paddy Francis stage-managed a lot of the shows and took a lot of the practical effort off Jim's shoulders. Fred was a lovely man too; perky, cheerful, always interested, always in good humour.

Like Der Donovan, many people of that generation used both the English and the Irish version of their names. For instance I was always Donal. All my family called me Donal till the day they died. 'Dan' occurred in school and stuck to me. Connie Buckley called me Dan.

Back to your dreams of founding Everyman.

In all my viewing year after year in London I was intensely preoccupied with the art of acting. There is no doubt that late-war and post-war London was a treasure house of acting. Maybe acting in the old style in which great players who have learnt their craft in repertory or any other way approached drama to present the text, often a text that tackled big themes, in a manner what would bring it spectacularly to life. I saw all the great actors: not only Redgrave but Olivier, Alec Guinness, Gielgud, Ralph Richardson and Trevor Howard.

Did you ever meet any of these actors?

I had one rather hilarious if 'wet' day with Trevor Howard during one of his many visits to Cork during the Film Festival. He was very partial to the gargle but was a most delightful man, modest and interesting. He told me an anecdote about John Willie Nolan, the ferryman to Sherkin Island where he was filming, so that I could remind him of it when I was presenting him on stage later. I'm afraid I quite forgot it when I was introducing him so I proved a dubious crutch for Trevor's memory, but there were mitigating circumstances.

People think of him in relation to the great days of Ryan's Daughter *(1971) in Dingle.*

Indeed they do. He loved working in Ireland. Some aspect of my desires to do these plays was based on the idea of imitating in my own tinpot way some of the qualities that I so adored in these people. I was very anxious that the whole tradition of theatre with a strong central emphasis on acting and presentation and text would not go to seed. And of course I wanted to keep a bit of imaginative life in my own theatre work because of the long runs and repeated revivals with STG.

John O'Shea had revived the UCC Dramatic Society. With Donall Farmer, who taught in Pres for a couple of years, he did an interesting production of *The Dumb Waiter* by Pinter and *The Mad Woman of Chaillot* by Giradoux. He did many interesting productions under the name of Cinque Productions. I knew him since he was at school in Pres and greatly admired his imaginative and ever-increasing interest in all matters theatrical. He came to us when his Alma Mater, Coláiste Chríost Rí here in Turner's Cross, also run by the Presentation Brothers, was moving from being a secondary top to a full-scale secondary school. There was a bridge period during which a number of Chríost Rí pupils came to Pres. He joined the staff of Chríost Rí and made an enormous contribution when he returned there.

I became aware that Ashton Productions under the direction of Rachel Burrows had begun and very nearly completed a survey of all the verse plays of W. B. Yeats. She had given an extraordinary performance as the medium through whom the voice of Swift spoke

The Burrows family in 1947.

in *The Words upon the Window Pane,* in one of the *Tóstals* which we discussed. She was widely interested in drama. She had been a pupil of Beckett's in Trinity and had notes[38] from his lectures. She had a powerful presence and a marvellous voice, added to a very deep feeling for everything connected with the theatre. She was the founder of the French Society and Betty was a member, so I knew of Rachel on many accounts. She taught French and English in the Cork Grammar School, now Ashton, where her husband was headmaster from 1947 until his retirement.

The other aspect of Everyman which involved both John and myself was Compántas Chorcaí, which was brought into the framework so that Irish plays would be a normal part of Everyman. This meant that a leading Irish dramatist, Seán Ó Tuama, was part of the Everyman movement. The objects of the movement were not purely theatrical but helped to serve the cause of this rising Irish dramatist, whose ambition it was to enliven the whole scene of Gaelic drama.

Naturally the PTG came within the fold of this amalgamation of companies. It shared many of the aims and functions that were common to all the theatre groups: presenting plays of quality both Irish and international in well-planned seasons. If you work on an amateur basis you have to take the haphazard, slipshod element out of it. We planned our programmes with careful reference to choice of play, making the selection as widely international as possible and doing plays that had not been presented in Cork before. We were very conscious of plugging gaps. Planning for the first season took a long time. It was a question of working out a programme. An enormous amount of credit goes to John O'Shea for his patience and marshalling of people. Most of the groups already had production arrangements and production teams available. We drew on the common pool of expertise available in the city, Pat Murray included. Ray Casey provided excellent lighting and Frank Fitzgerald did many fine sets.

The first blessing we had was the little 100-seater theatre in Castle Street which had been refurbished by the Catholic Young Mens' Society and was a perfect venue for the sort of plays that we proposed to attempt. That allowed us to plan a season from September to June. Rent was reasonable. We had a certain time for rehearsal but we couldn't rehearse there much. The Brothers very kindly allowed me to rehearse in Pres. Likewise Rachel rehearsed in Ashton. In the first couple of seasons we still more or less retained our earlier group identities: 'Everyman Theatre presents PTG in such and such a play.' I did *Tidings Brought to Mary* for PTG in that way. Gradually a united Everyman company came into existence and we ceased to be a series of one group bands. There was an increasing sense of solidarity and an increasing sense of excitement at what was beginning to unfold under our hands.

Everyman was founded in that epic year, 1963. The collective Cork memory of President Kennedy coming to Cork that summer is still strong.

The Kennedy thing certainly created an enormous stir. For the first time someone like that was, as it were, almost coming home to us. The excitement had built up because of all we had seen and heard about all the other places he had visited, not just Dublin but Wexford for example. We were intensely aware of the character of the man and looking forward to his getting the Freedom of the City. He was to get it from Seán Casey, the Lord Mayor of the time and a good friend of mine from Pres days. Every place in Cork was a stepping stone towards the event. There was a big movement of people in towards the city all through the morning. It was a very nice day. I remember I walked in from Turner's Cross. I came down over Parliament Street Bridge onto South Mall. I got a vantage point for myself there because I knew the cavalcade would pass on its way to City Hall. There was a little delay with a general atmosphere of hushed

Crowds cheer President John F. Kennedy in Cork.

excitement, a real sense of occasion. One of the nice things about all that had gone before this was a certain homeliness in the welcome. The natural warmth Kennedy generated himself was reciprocated. He came among us as one of our own. We were flattered by this. Eventually police outriders came along. Then came the cavalcade. We saw the great man and with his usual charismatic smile, there was a genuine sense of being greeted almost personally by him as he passed by. The grandees were in City Hall. As I didn't have much influence in those days I had no entrée to City Hall.

So I decided to retire to Joe Kealy's pub and watch the TV. It was on Faulkener's Lane leading to the Crawford Gallery. TV was still a novelty then. There were a lot of TV sets already purchased in Cork but I certainly didn't have one. They were by no means universal. I had no objection to spending an hour or two in the genial company of mine host Joe Kealy. Joe later left Cork and went to Dublin, where he set up another flourishing business in the licensed trade somewhere near the airport. He was an excellent publican with fine standards and a lovely premises. He had a strong midlands accent. He had a range of cold meats, freshly cut and hygienically handled, and soup of course. I was partial to a bit of Danish Blue. Joe would say 'And a bit of Danish Blue to round it off, Mr Donovan?' Manners were very proper in those days. There were conventions about talking to people. If you were addressed aloud across a room you'd be called 'Mr So-and-So'. If you were man-to-man it might be 'Joe' or 'Dan'. At any kind of public address you were 'Mr'. A false familiarity was a little bit frowned upon then. Even Professor Fleischmann never called me anything but 'Mr Donovan'. The only time he ever broke that with me was when there was a bit of an emergency once and he rushed across the room, saying rather anxiously 'Has Dan arrived yet?'

On TV I was delighted to see my old schoolmate Seán Casey head and tail of the ceremony and to see the great man in our midst. I almost felt I was in City Hall. The departure when he came out was very crowded. It was civic theatre for Cork on the grandest scale. Everyone who was anyone was there. I remember Mrs Jenny Dowdall, an ample, jovial and articulate woman who played an important part in civic life for many years. She was very encouraging of all the arts, particularly the ballet. Finbarr, her son, was later prominent in cultural life in Cork and ran the family business of O'Dowdall O'Mahony. Peter Barry's father would have been there. Cork was better off than many parts of the country then. The shipping business was still extensive and Ford and Dunlop gave a lot of employment. The big fertiliser plant Gouldings were still there. There was a rich hinterland. Hence there were great crowds waiting outside City Hall to greet the new Freeman.

The 1960s – what a rich decade for Cork theatre, with Seán Ó Tuama and John B. and Everyman taking off and literary censorship declining.[37]

In no time at all we in Everyman had well-planned seasons with a pool of actors drawn from all the groups. The early seasons of Everyman seem to have passed like a dream or a nightmare because in addition to working in the Southern Theatre Group, I played Frank Elgin, a failed alcoholic actor in *The Country Girl*. Donall Farmer played the director/producer. Bernie Holland (née Neiland) played the female role, originally played by Googie Withers, whom I saw in it in London. This play was revived for the fortieth anniversary of Everyman in the Everyman Palace Theatre and directed by Michael Twomey. All except Billy Newman who sadly died the year before, were at the revival of that first Everyman production.

We had a programme of four one-act plays, *Quartet. Tidings Brought to Mary* was a version of the famous religious play by Paul Claudel, a rather remarkable verse play in its treatment of suffering and almost mystical religious power. Miss O'Flaherty in College translated an

Dan Donovan, Bernie Holland, Donall Farmer, Irene Comerford outside the Everyman Palace Theatre, 2003.

act for me. She was a thorough expert and knew, revised and tightened the play. She later became professor of French. There we were drawing on willing help and co-operation from all sources. Some saviours always came to help.

John O'Shea did *Thieves Carnival* by Jean Anouilh and *Sergeant Musgrave's Dance,* a very colourful and imaginative production of John Arden's play. It is a very strong anti-war play. John Arden and his wife were very radical in their approach. I had a delightful little cameo part as the Bargee.

Dan as the Bargee in Sergeant Musgrave's Dance, *c. 1963.*

In a north of England play like this, parts like the Bargee's are very robust. What I often felt about my voice was that when I was young, I was always playing people much older than myself. In fact I was aware that I could handle lighter and more delicate parts, taking great pleasure in being economical and disciplined with my vocal resources. For instance in *The Black Stranger* with PTG, I played the part of Seán the Fool, based on a *duine le Dia,* a simpleton that I knew who used to ramble around Ballincollig mentioning the most ordinary things in the most wonderstruck and imaginative way. It could be something as commonplace as 'Fr Sexton has gone up the road.' But he said it with a sense of sheer wonder. I realised that he gave me a key into the performance. I wasn't worried about the more delicate nuances required in acting certain parts. Broadcasting made me aware of the necessity of getting the disembodied voice to create the impression of the solidity and fullness of the character whose physical reality would create quite a different impression on stage. But I was in danger of imitating or using as a model maybe people like Gielgud or Mac Liammóir and was sometimes accused critically of overusing the 'voice beautiful'. This was most likely to happen in plays which had rather old-fashioned, fine writing in them. To tell the truth fine writing was always a bit of a temptation for me. The worst dangers of that were avoided for me by the fact that I had quite a good sense of dialect. In something like *Sergeant Musgrave's Dance* I don't think there was any danger of a prissy vocal presentation by the Bargee damaging the robustness of the character. John's production of this brought the first Everyman season to a strong and powerful finish.

There was no doubt that there would be a second Everyman season in 1964–65. The end of the season didn't mean the end of work because play reading became essential. We had to retain the range and variety of our programme and of course we had to pay attention to problems of casting. It wasn't possible or desirable for every actor to be available for every play. The planning was a very constant business. John cracked the whip and kept us busy reading and putting forward plans that might work and be readily cast. We might use the French Acting Editions. We began to develop a good deal with Loreta MacNamara in Captain Feehan's Mercier Bookshop on 4 Bridge Street. Loreta was very good at ferreting out scripts. Or we would get them from libraries. One of the bugbears of my life was to work with old typewritten scripts in the Gestetner copies. It wasn't always easy to put together a set of legible scripts. We very often had to get them typed at great expense.

John's brother Aidan was coming steadily into the picture as a rising young actor and director. John, Rachel, Donall Farmer and I worked closely, until Donall left Cork to join the Radio Éireann rep and trained as a professional TV director. This kind of thing sadly became a problem. We began to lose our very good people regularly, year in, year out. Young people fortunately were always emerging.

Ó Tuama's weren't the only Irish language plays you did, were they?

No. For example, in Irish we also did Brendan Behan's *An Giall* which later became *The Hostage* in London. *The Hostage* was a monster created by Joan Littlewood from Behan's original rather simpler Irish play. Behan had nice Irish.

Aidan O'Shea in The Fire Raisers, *1965.*

Didn't his uncle Peadar Kearney, a theatre man, write the National Anthem?

Yes, he did. John O'Shea did a splendid selection of post-war European plays, including *The Fire Raisers* by the dramatist, Max Frisch. Again as with *Moloney, The Fire Raisers* in an iconic sort of way presented the gradual rise of Nazism in a climate that was unaware of its menace. I played the lead, Biederman, who is the ordinary, tolerant guy who calmly and smugly accepts the national socialists – the fire raisers – into his home and shuts his eyes to the damage gathering around him, until the final confrontation emerges.

While this interest in war-related plays was strong, you favoured a wide range of plays?

Yes. I had experienced Polish culture through reading some of their poets and was pleased when the Wajda *Ashes and Diamonds* trilogy with the young Polish actor Cybulski was shown in the Film Festival. He became known in Cork through partaking in so many post-war films. Sadly this young actor, a star, perished in a railway accident. He was extremely short-sighted and stepped off a platform in front of a train in Warsaw, shortly after his appearance in the Film Festival in 1958 or 1959.

The central European post-war experience resonated deeply with me when I read the collected plays of Mrozek. Mrozek represented the central European experience which used but adapted some of the traditional forms of theatre for the changed post-war experience. We did two programmes of Polish plays, Mrozek's *Tango* and a double bill with *The Police* and *Out at Sea* in the early 1970s. They were Theatre of the Absurd plays. Bob Crowley designed and I directed. *Tango* was a mid-European version of *Hamlet* really. The pressures in the Shakespearean play were worked out in terms of the current European situation. I saw *Tango* in London with Michael Williams in the lead. These plays were part of the climate of the time and grew up out of the wartime experiences and the changes in society and in theatrical reflections of that society in a way that marked a radical change from pre-war theatre. *The Police* deals with authoritarianism and the clash between the freedom of the spirit and the restrictions that obtained. *Out at Sea* is a delightful little one-act play where four or five people are isolated in a boat. Plays at the time seemed to concentrate on a small group in a desperate situation. But in *Out at Sea* Mrozek presented it in a very humorous manner. I made a spectacular dive off the boat.

Our own experience in Ireland was isolated from that wartime experience. It seemed very important to me to bring an artistic expression of the horrors of world war home to our Irish consciousness. Whatever our own complaints, we missed that horror.

One night when I was presenting in City Hall during a Choral Festival, just as I was about to announce a visiting choir, a young man dashed onto the stage, seized the microphone and proceeded to address the audience about Ireland's troubles. Luckily I had a master switch and was able to cut off the sound. He was followed by two Special Branch men who whipped him off the stage. Someone said to me afterwards 'Was that a part of the show?' I said 'No, it was a slightly upsetting incident.' It showed the peculiar mindset that imagined that people who had been through the horrors of the War all over Europe could conceivably sympathise with efforts to promote Ireland's cause as in any way comparable to the hell they'd just been through.

We did favour a wide range of plays, from the beginning. The second Everyman season, in 1964–5, involved a collaboration with the Cork Orchestral Society and the Ballet Company to do Purcell's *Fairy Queen* in City Hall. People were surprised it was not based solidly on Spenser's *Faerie Queene,* which was dedicated to Queen Elizabeth 1. Pat Murray did the set. This was the second Purcell *Fairy Queen* which we did. I took responsibility for the production this time, keeping the reins of power in my own hands, as the first time there had been rather too many directors. This big collaborative project with singers and dancers inevitably cast light on the passing years. In 1947–48, in the earlier production, I played Oberon the King opposite Lorna Daly's Titania – Purcell's libretto is based on Shakespeare's *A Midsummer Night's Dream.* I had rather a come-down in the Everyman 1964 production, in which I played Billy Bottom the weaver!

What about Beckett? Did Cork theatre folk of your generation, apart from Rachel, like putting on Beckett?

I remember talking to Jim Stack after one of our classes in the School of Music about Beckett and he said the Theatre of the Absurd came too late for him. I was just about young enough to take Beckett into my stride. Rachel's interest in Beckett was very inspiring. I played in *Krapp's Last Tape* directed by John O'Shea in the early 1970s.

Did you like the voice of Patrick Magee, for whom Beckett wrote the part?

Yes, I did. I think some people thought his Northern accent was too strong. Magee had a very appropriate and sensitive tone for the nuances and pausings, the skilful timings that Beckett's complex verbal patterns required. Though I had done *Waiting for Godot* (1949), I found the whole verbal patterning of *Krapp's Last Tape* particularly satisfying, with the challenge of preserving the immediacy of the practical business of the play with the tape recorder and the constantly changing world of memory that had to be created in the living moment. I recall enjoying the performing of Krapp in the late 1960s or early 1970s, except for one evening when a certain amount of tension was added to a performance. John O'Shea always carefully monitored the business of the tape recorder with a second machine offstage but that evening he ran into some difficulties with the controls, leaving my recorded voice from the past totally absent. John muttered 'Dan, Dan keep going.' I don't think Sam would have appreciated my efforts to compensate. It seemed an eternity but John's voice eventually came through: 'Carry on Dan, we're back on track.'

In the 1968–9 season I had my first Beckett production with *Waiting for Godot*. It had been done in the CYMS with Nigel Fitzgerald in the 1950s. He was a big man and played a very good Pozzo. It was a transfer from Dublin. We had an excellent cast for the Everyman *Godot*, with Pat Butler – who later had a very good career as director, producer and presenter in Radio Éireann – the young Noel Murphy, Albert Cole and, if I may say so, myself as Pozzo. It was nicely set by Frank Fitzgerald, who worked as a meteorologist in the airport, and was a great success.

The Everyman cast in **Waiting for Godot.** *l–r: Dan Donovan, Noel Murphy, Pat Butler, Albert Cole.*

I did *Endgame* with Rachel and Michael McCarthy and Albert Cole. Albert had a pharmacy in Youghal and was a semi-founder of Everyman. He was a tremendously active leader of the Youghal Dramat, who through him became very closely associated with the establishment of Everyman. He became one of our finest and most loyal actors and directors. Rachel had a regular group including Albert whom she instructed in the techniques of theatre verse speaking, when over several seasons she produced all the Yeats plays at Ashton and other venues.

Didn't the young Pinter play in the lovely theatre in Youghal?

Yes. He worked with Anew McMaster and wrote a lovely tribute to him.

Wasn't Rachel, like Geraldine Neeson, interesting in the way she combined motherhood and her theatre interests?

She was married to Canon Jerome Burrows and their home in Cork

Rachel Burrows.

was like a literary salon of the old days. Rachel was tremendously welcoming. And even though she had a family of daughters [Margaret and Mary], encouraged by Jerome she did great work. Jerome was tall, thin and extremely kindly and understanding; qualities which were occasionally rather necessary when dealing with some of Rachel's bohemian guests. Early one morning when repairing to the bathroom to shave in preparation for the day's chores at Ashton, he encountered a strange man on the landing. It was the pianist Charles Lynch, to whom Rachel had given a bed. Jerome politely greeted him and passed on his way without comment. Rachel in the charity of her big heart was always ready to help out with board and lodging for any passing waif or stray. Everyone from the various companies in Cork went to their house, the Ballet Company included. Pat Murray would be there, often to rather late hours. She had another wonderfully hospitable home in Kilbaha in County Clare. She was a Dobbin from Clare. When Jerome retired they went to Dublin and she became a professional actress for a time. I remember her playing Lady Bracknell in the Opera House in a touring production of *The Importance of Being Earnest*.

What was theatre in Cork like when the Opera House re-opened in 1965?

Circumstances once again began to change as the Opera House was nearing completion. An awful lot of theatre in Cork since it burnt down ten years earlier was an adaptation to its loss. Southern Theatre Group for example had done most of its work inevitably in the Father Mathew Hall. All the great early Keanes were done there. And now the Opera House would become a venue once more, taking from the lesser venues temporarily used. For example, Theatre of the South, with its large audiences and success with the Keane plays, would inevitably go to the Opera House stage, however unsuitable the large stage was to the kind of play we were presenting. It could, you know, be a rather dreary place if you didn't have a full audience. It was designed to answer all demands from the one-man show to a big opera. But having successfully presented two seasons, Everyman had no intention of moving from the CYMS when the Opera House re-opened.

The authorities who owned and ran the little theatre in Castle Street, the Catholic Young Men's Society, a Catholic social club involving billiard rooms, card rooms and general facilities on a social level, principally for the middle parish of St Peter's and Paul's, gave us special privileges in terms of bookings and other matters. As far as I can remember most of the men weren't that young, as the population of the city had started to become very widely scattered to the various housing developments outside the city centre. I have to pay tribute to the kindness and support of the committee. Jim Ryan was one of the people who bent over backwards to help and encourage us. They were delighted that we had become a successful operation and much of that success was due to their kindly co-operation. The stage was basically equipped. We were able to provide some extra sound and lighting as required. Downstairs there was an old gym and some outbuildings where we were able to store a certain amount of scenery and properties. Like the Father Mathew Hall, it was rented by others also, so that problems of get-out arose after productions quite often. I can recall one night where I found myself on a ladder taking down some electric spots, with electrician Ray Casey down the hall on another and John O'Shea and Donall Farmer on stage clearing away the old set. So there were practical drawbacks. But they seemed very small, and surmountable.

One of the problems for us in view of the ambitious choice of plays with large casts was the cramped onstage facilities. The building curved from South Main Street around to Castle Street so there was practically no wing space on the right. On the left there was a steep stairway leading down to the gym and one dressing room below. It was a rather dangerous stairway. Audiences entered up a wider stairs from Castle Street. There was a kind of a trade entrance from South Main Street. The depth of the stage was quite shallow. John O'Shea's *Sergeant Musgrave's Dance* had a large cast and I wondered at the miracles of movement and crowd control exercised by John's inventive skills.

Near the end of a performance of Denis Johnston's Swift play *The*

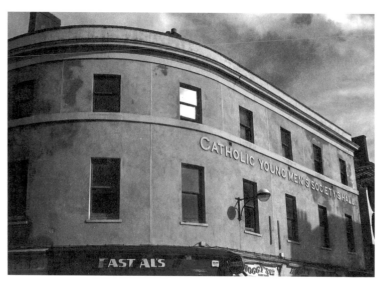

Catholic Young Men's Society Hall, Castle Street/South Main Street, Cork, 2007.

Dreaming Dust, I was watching in the wings with one of the cast, and there was a bit of a hiatus in the performance. The man next to me, a great old trooper acting one of the small parts said 'Well, typical, typical. So-and-so is missing his cue again.' The stage manager suddenly came rushing up and said to him, 'Billy, you're on, you're on.' He was jet-propelled onto the stage and the hiatus ceased. In Castle Street you had to place yourself on the side where you were entering or else go up a very tricky ladder across the top of the stage. I had a ball playing Dean Swift in *The Dreaming Dust.* I also directed. It had a large cast and worked quite well. Rachel played in that. She was back in a very familiar area, having done *The Words upon the Window Pane,* also about Swift, earlier. Denis Johnston wrote *The Old Lady Says 'No',* one of the most famous of the Edwards and Mac Liammóir productions at the Gate shortly after it opened.

Looking back, the CYMS was free of any kind of constricting regulation and was one of the happiest phases of my working life in the theatre. Maybe because of its limitations of size it had an extra-compelling atmosphere. It had a unique, warm spirit that imbued the theatre itself and everyone who worked in it and attended it. The famous three 'A's – author, actor and audience – seemed to merge in a unified way.

I had used the CYMS already when the old Assembly Hall which became the CYMS theatre was converted at some cost to the committee. Of course it had been available to the PTG. It was within easy walking distance of the school. For example, we had put on Thornton Wilder's *Our Town* there. The Clopet–Yorke group, exiled from the old Opera House, had several seasons there before moving to the Father Mathew Hall. So the use of the place had been pioneered for us by 1963.

After my exertions in the opening seasons I cut back my activities for the next two seasons. I was involved in two American plays for the third. I acted in and directed William Inge's play *Come Back, Little Sheba*. Having started the first season with a play about an alcoholic I found myself returning to the role in Inge's delicate and nicely written play. I helped with the production of Tennessee Williams' *Summer and Smoke* which was directed by Máire Nic Lochlainn, 'Locky' as she was called. For the fourth season I came back to Ireland and did a new Irish play by Seán Ó Drisceoil, *Tycoon*. It was a sign we were not totally dependent on Seán Ó Tuama. I acted the tycoon. It's about a self-made businessman, a figure that was of considerable interest at the time, illustrating how Irish business life was developing in ways that were capable of being criticised sometimes.

We talked earlier about Seán Ó Tuama's play *Judas Iscariot agus a Bhean*, a very demanding play which I directed for the fifth Everyman season in 1967–8. I also played Judas the actor having a nervous breakdown and was nearly having a nervous breakdown myself. It had premiered in Dublin. As a relief after the rigours of Judas, I had a lovely, joint cameo part in John O'Shea's production *A Scent of Flowers*, in which I played two of the parts involving a death: the priest – again – at the funeral Mass and the rather poncey undertaker in charge of the more material side of interment. I had fun with that. My last production for the fifth Everyman season was Ibsen's *Hedda Gabler*. Máirín Murphy, afterwards one of those who succeeded Stackey in the School of Music, played Hedda.

As the 1960s came to a close many changes which we must discuss were coming about, but let's hear more about other Everyman productions in CYMS please.

My personal contribution to our main purpose, to consolidate the successful presentation of a series of pre-planned programmes with six plays chosen and selected for each season, was fairly extensive. In one way or another, in the first two seasons, I was involved in nine of the twelve productions. Demands were made on certain people to a very heavy degree. But certainly the steady contributions of so many regular members of the company gave a consistency of range and effort that in fact characterised the entire period in Castle Street. My involvement began to lessen a little.

The seventh Everyman season, 1969–70, was an extremely busy one for me, almost as busy as the first and second. I played in one of the few Shavian productions we did, *You Never Can Tell*, directed by John. I then followed one of my own strong interests, verse theatre, and did one of T. S. Eliot's most difficult plays, *The Cocktail Party*.

I had splendid performances from Rachel, Marion Cullinane, [née King], a superb actress and, all in all, a very even cast. The central part I played myself but I found the demands of directing and acting were beginning to take their toll by then. I was delighted to be able to do it but I was aware that I was unlikely to attempt anything like it again. As a play it is a little remote from the ordinary experience. One critic suggested that the doctor in it is probably best explained as an effort to represent God, testing the meaning of suffering and fate at a level that transcends ordinary reality. It tries to deal with mystical experience and the meaning of human experience. A lot of the dilemmas Eliot explored, as he tried to find through the medium of verse and poetic exposition a spiritual reality, had been powerfully stimulated by his conversion to Anglicanism. I later had the pleasure of directing a good cast in *The Family Reunion* in Father Mathew Hall. I had done *Murder in the Cathedral* in Pres and in the Opera House. So I got three of the Eliots in. I was a bit of a completist.

That season I did one of the best productions I ever did, Jean Anouilh's *The Waltz of the Toreadors*, with a superb cast including Rachel. She didn't like the part as the awful wife of the General but she was superb in it. Elaine Stevens and Michael McCarthy were also superb. But for some reason we had to postpone it for a week or so. So

Dan Donovan and Marion King in The Cocktail Party, *1969.*

it went on into June of 1970 to a heatwave and very small audiences. It was one of the most completely successful things I did and was seen by very few. The responsible director usually provided his own funding for the production as a kind of an investment, which he would hope to get back. I'm afraid with royalties and a very careful production I lost a lot of money, something that could happen occasionally. But support was usually buoyant enough and

Betty Donovan.

losses small enough. Strangely, I recouped my losses in the 1971–2 season with *Endgame* and *Krapp's Last Tape*.

One of our American actresses, Susan Milch, played in the production of Tennessee Williams's *Cat on a Hot Tin Roof*, with Pat Butler and Marion King. Sue's husband was in business in Kinsale. Her American accent maybe pointed out some of the deficiencies of our own. That season was concluded with a bang. Donall Farmer came back as a guest performer for Anouilh's *Poor Bitos*, attended in Castle Street by the French ambassador, Vicomte d'Harcourt. Betty was secretary for years to the Cork French Society so she was very pleased. I think I played a revolutionary – Danton maybe. The French were anxious to mark their participation in the production of this historical play. Before we joined the Common Market in 1957, boys were rarely taught French. My French was very poor and so I relied on Betty and Rachel to do the honours on this glamorous occasion. They did so with the utmost elegance and panache.

9

A Palace Regained

Everyman moved to the Father Mathew Hall in the early 1970s.

The 1960s proved to be one of the busiest times of my theatrical career and life in general. Life itself was changing, teaching was changing. I suppose in retrospect it was a little bit unwise of me in terms of time and energy to get so heavily involved with the commercial operation of Southern Theatre Group and also continue to direct and act in the sort of theatre I had grown used to in the old PTG, enshrined in the early 1960s in the newly founded Everyman. Adding to the teaching, Southern Theatre Group was making such heavy demands because of the extraordinary success of the John B. Keane plays, with their long runs, frequent seasons and the inspiring demands of work that was new and exciting. The old human vanity came into play and I didn't want to let it go, or let go of the possibilities of doing on a regular basis some of the interesting, contemporary plays or indeed the great classics that I had grown used to attempting. This dilemma in terms of workload I solved in the usual way, by ignoring it. I think I got away with it for the seasons in the CYMS.

But the cracks began to show. The end of the Castle Street era and the return to Father Mathew Hall in the early 1970s meant that the practical demands of mounting plays were becoming quite severe. I remember Liam St John Devlin, chair of CIÉ and from a well-known

Cork family, giving us enormous help with the changeover. The three Everyman directors in Castle Street were Seán Ó Tuama, John O'Shea and myself. Seán decided to retire, as academic demands and his work in the Irish language movement were increasing. Personally, I deeply missed Seán. His going was a loss to everyone because of the quality of his creative contribution in terms of those marvellous original

John O'Shea.

plays, so successful and creating such prestige for the Everyman Company. We were helped by the fact that Leachlain Ó Cathain from Compántas Chorcaí replaced Seán. Leachlain with his practical skills as a solicitor was able to contribute to the expanding company in very many ways. Leachlain, like Seán, was deeply involved in the language revival movement. John O'Shea organised the company very effectively. He was good at getting supports and organising the theatrical strengths in the various ways required from script reading to auditions. The demands had to be spread. What was becoming clear was that an extra dimension of professional involvement was necessary. The local directors were increased in number.

We were hardworking people with our own jobs. For years we could do it. We carried on reading scripts and planning seasons. But now there was the whole business of running a decent-sized theatre. The Father Mathew Hall, now the Everyman Playhouse, had in excess of 400 seats. We were encouraged, probably by Liam St John Devlin, to apply for help from the Arts Council. Originally quite a small grant was given by the Arts Council to deal with practical matters arising from the operation of the Playhouse which had to be managed on a hands-on basis. There were a few tentative efforts at organising that. Pat Fleming, until he left us to go to the Opera House, gave excellent help as did an Englishman Peter Bell, a professional theatre man who was there for a year or two. In fact the solution to our problem came with the appointment of Donn McMullin, who for the next ten years excellently and with real flair managed the practical side of the Everyman Playhouse in Father Mathew Hall. The Arts Council were not prepared to subsidise any of what they called amateur theatre in the Everyman Playhouse. They would only act as an enabling agent to finance professional administration relating to the box office and routine matters of a theatre venue which was receiving touring shows from professional companies. The professional companies were a strong part of the Arts Council's policy and had to be provided with a properly managed venue. While we co-operated as fully as we could and were delighted to get increased grants, we were presented with real dilemmas.

For example, the great civic showpiece for Cork was the annual Father Mathew *Feis*. It was like the *Feis Ceoil* in Dublin and was increasingly expanding in range and in the demands it made on the time of both the Everyman Playhouse management and of course the actual owners of the Father Mathew Hall, the Capuchins. They had founded and continued to run the *Feis* most successfully. There were frequent difficulties when tours backed by the Arts Council couldn't be slotted in to the schedules in Father Mathew Hall. It was the Father Mathew Hall to the owners and the Everyman Playhouse to us. There were sensitivities we respected. The Tom Murphy play, *The J. Arthur Maginnis Story,* had a reference to Father Mathew that presented us with a little dilemma. From our angle, in relation to having a licence to play in Father Mathew Hall, it was in dubious taste. Between the *Feis* and the problem in relation to Father Mathew, Murphy's play was not presented by Everyman. Very often plays might have reference to matters that could be regionally sensitive and no such problem would occur when produced in the capital.

The Irish Theatre Company would have been one of the big touring companies. They came right through the 1970s. The Abbey came right through the 1970s and 1980s. Field Day Productions came a few times; we had *The Riot Act* and Friel's *The Communication Cord*. Gemini came too. We organised these visits but inevitably while we could select dates for our own productions in the Father Mathew Hall, the *Feis* meant there was a huge block of unavailable time during the spring season. We found ourselves increasingly concerned with dealing with the venue and the conflict between our own Everyman needs, Arts Council policy and the basic requirements of the theatre ownership.

Everyman was essentially a community theatre, an organisation which grew up in friendship and collaboration and now we found ourselves frequently involved in difficulties caused by the strict requirements of the Arts Council, who in no way would countenance subsidising amateur work. On a practical basis we managed pretty well. We took the chewing gum off the seats after Bingo and swept the floor when we were there and Brother Paul tucked up his bib and did it when we were not. The Capuchins were very helpful to us. After the Opera House re-opened in 1965, Everyman Playhouse helped to replace the companies who returned there. Southern Theatre Group and other companies used the Father Mathew Hall, the largest venue in Cork after the Opera House burnt down.

We became rather fixated by problems of the venue and the situation was not to improve during our continued residence there. I feel our eye went off the ball as regards the more literary and creative sides of theatre. All the hassle made us neglect the necessity to replace Seán Ó Tuama. Maybe we should have been sharper at finding some new writers who would have helped us to maintain that necessary creative

Michael Twomey and Dan Donovan, 1992.

aspect of the company's earlier work. But *ní thagann an dá thrá leis an gobadán*; the sandpiper can't work the two strands. I think our regional creativity and independence were being seriously eroded. My contention is that this was showing itself quite early on in the seasons at the Everyman Playhouse. That we were able to work there for ten or twelve years was in no small way due to Donn's expertise and the goodwill he generated in the venue. He was an actor, a producer, a director; he was everything. He got on well with theatrical people and created a splendid atmosphere. He had been manager with the Irish Ballet Company for a few years before he came to Everyman in or about 1976.

Pat Murray as a set designer had reached his full maturity, displaying extraordinary versatility in every challenge that he undertook. But it was extraordinary again that a small theatrical movement in a city like Cork could nurture another amazing talent. During our early years in the Hall, Bob Crowley, who like Pat had attended the Crawford School of Art, began to reveal his gifts. As I was saying he designed for the Mrozek plays that I directed, *The Police* and *Out at Sea* in the tenth Everyman season, 1973–1974.

He designed many wonderful posters, including the one for *The Plough and the Stars*. That season, in Michael Twomey's production of *Death of a Salesman,* I fulfilled a long-term ambition and played the salesman, Willy Loman. This production transferred to the Opera House. Frank Fitzgerald did the set for *Death of a Salesman* (1948) but I do believe Bob designed the poster. The salesman's face on it is mine and it is crossed by dark and light diagonal lines. David McInerney, another of our strong actors and singers, playfully remarked that the strong black diagonals represent Dan Donovan when he remembers his lines and the dim diagonals represent him when he forgot them. Bob of course was to leave in a short time for the international career which has brought him such fame. That fame reflects

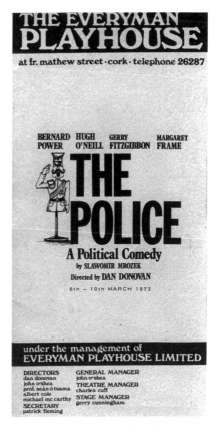

Bob Crowley's programme for The Police.

happily on our early days. Young people were coming up. I directed Pat Talbot in a revival of *Gunna Cam* in 1980. Pat was becoming very prominent among the younger members of Everyman. He had been a pupil of John O'Shea's in Coláiste Chríost Rí and was, very early on, deeply inspired by John's readings of the great dramatic texts. Pat became an effective director and actor and is now in charge of Everyman Palace Theatre, doing a splendid job both in terms of management and artistic direction. Fiona Shaw was already well known as a fine actor when she was a student in UCC. John worked

EVERYMAN PLAYHOUSE

ARTHUR MILLER'S

DEATH OF A SALESMAN

OPENING
JAN 30

DIRECTED BY
MICHAEL TWOMEY
DESIGNED BY
FRANK FITZGERALD

Everyman poster for **Death of a Salesman.**

with her. I didn't succeed in doing so. When I went back to Dramat in UCC to do a guest production of *St Joan*, a very successful one, at the invitation of Ger Fitzgibbon, she was alas unavailable for rehearsal.

Splendid work was done in the Father Mathew Hall. During the eleventh Everyman season, in 1974–5, I was involved in two splendid productions, neither of which I directed myself. I played Norfolk in John O'Shea's blockbuster of Robert Bolt's *A Man for All Seasons*. Brendan Fehily was a magnificent Thomas More. In 1980, I again played in another Michael Twomey production of Arthur Miller. I played the father in *All My Sons*. I had previously done it in the CYMS with the PTG. I found the whole social context of Miller's plays enormously stimulating, even though they dealt with a different cultural background to ours. They were as relevant in an Irish context as they were in the original American context.

For a man socially involved who had a deep conscience, Miller did not advert in his memoirs[40] very clearly to the fact that there was a son problem in his life. I found it very shocking to think that a man of his calibre, with so much understanding and tenderness of heart, could almost gloss over the fact that he had rejected a son, who could perhaps have been helped by a father's care. Down's syndrome children become very lovable when love is shown to them on a regular basis.

You seem to have engaged very deeply with 'father' plays.

As we discussed earlier, I lost my father in 1935 when I was nine years of age and I think I felt a great gap in my life when that happened. I recall vividly being at home one Saturday morning. I seem to have been alone in the house. All the others, being older, had gone to the South Infirmary. I recall daydreaming in my little room. At about eleven o'clock Tim came home. He found me. I always remember the way he broke it to me. He said 'Donal' – that was my family name – 'I'm afraid Dad won't be coming home to Ballincollig any more.' I knew my father was ill but I didn't know what death meant. There was a bit of a silence around his illness. I had visited him in the South Infirmary of course. Looking back on it I see he was very drawn and weak. I almost set aside the signs of weakness and saw him as he had been. He was a great gardener. I often assisted him with gardening. He was always pottering around the house, always there in a quiet, managing, supportive kind of a way.

Recently I began to recall one of the only rows I ever witnessed between my mother and father. One day when he had come into Cork to pick up his pension, he collected me from Pres. We went to meet his old cronies in a pub on Oliver Plunkett Street, near the bus station on Grand Parade. He had a couple of pints and met a few magpies that day. His luck was not in. He delayed a little longer. The conversation was going high. I was bloated with lemonade. Lo and behold, having collected me in the afternoon didn't we miss the six o'clock bus, which meant we didn't get home to my mother until nine o'clock. We arrived in. He was very sheepish. She was upset and a bit furious. It was the only time she attacked him for keeping me out. Both instances were instances of caring. Their relationship was very close. That was a memory that I recalled peculiarly powerfully later on in life. It was the secret from my mother that went wrong. Our going to the pub meant that there was a sense of mischief shared outside the rules of the household, adding a little zest to what amounted to an adventure, where I met my father's old RIC buddies. That introduced me to some of the people who were important to the working life he had had. I never knew him as a member of the RIC. Alone with my brother that Saturday morning I sensed that a phase of my life was over.

There were signs that my mother continued to be upset after he died. For instance we left the house in Station Road and moved to our cousins' house, the Murphys, at the east end of the village for about four years. In 1939 we moved back to one of the teachers' residences. There were visible signs of her distress. Her blood pressure was getting higher. She felt a desire to return to where her married life had been. We had been in the middle residence and now we had the lower one. The excitement of the change was great but increasingly I think she was under strain. My father's absence was a continued presence, as it were. His pension, such as it was, had been an important factor in the household. In those days two incomes coming into a household was a rare enough thing. My brother's university career slowed down and I think she was increasingly worried about the future, with the calm, quiet, dignified presence of my father, a rock of support, gone.

That explains a good deal of the preoccupations in my theatre work: an acute sense of the instability of married life, for example, and the feeling of the loss of powerful props that could not be replaced. That led to a strong sense of the need to be independent and look after your own welfare. Looking back on it, that affected my attitude very strongly. Obviously the lack of a real father tended to make me look at the notion of fatherhood and the role of fatherhood in the life of a growing man. I'm struck for example by the way I responded strongly in choice of play and in the performances I was able to give of fathers, as if I was anxious to explore that role, without as it were desiring to move into that vulnerable role myself. In acting and directing, you experience all the tensions, all the types: good fathers, bad fathers, the relations that can be domineering. I think the two fathers in Miller – the bad, unfaithful husband in *Death of a Salesman* and the father who has misbehaved seriously in his work leading to all kinds of tensions in *All My Sons* and all the illnesses that can gather around families – are caught by Miller for his own reasons. I think most observers would say I was probably better in those parts than in any others. Nature and life had done a great deal of preparatory work for me.

Likewise *Hobson's Choice*, where a drunken father with two daughters has family conflict, particularly with the marriage of the bossy daughter, played so splendidly by Gerry McLoughlin in the Everyman production, to Willy Mossup equally splendidly acted by Michael McCarthy. This play is a complete contrast to the American play except for the basic theme of conflict. It is one of the fine, solid, rock-firm dramas of real life in the north of England tradition. A comic view was involved, which addressed a strong part of my temperament, a sense of humour. This was another of John O'Shea's splendid productions. I played the father in *The Barretts of Wimpole Street*, Rudolf Besier's play dealing with the romance between Elizabeth Barrett and Robert Browning, both poets. The father totally disapproves of the match. There's a whiff of incest in the play. As a matter of fact, B. G. MacCarthy had written her MA thesis on Browning and it was published with the rather grand title of *The Psychology of Genius*.[41]

The ultimate in my experience of fatherhood was playing the husband in Strindberg's *The Father* in which the poor Captain literally ends up in a straitjacket, thanks, as he feels it, to the machinations of his wife. Playing in and producing *The Father* was my only contribution to Everyman's final season in Castle Street in 1973. I was driving myself

Dan in Strindberg's The Father.

mad with some of my choices of plays but at last got it out of my system, with the help of Rosemary Archer who powerfully collaborated.

I'm conscious in old age that I covered up the vulnerability of the loss of my father and mother by being almost overactive, being stuck in everything: theatre and school work. I suppose my own experience of all these father roles was ultimately a healing exploration of those difficulties that arose in my childhood.

In practice the actual business of rehearsals and mounting plays was often fraught with personal danger for members of the cast.

Propinquity is a dangerous business. And, in fact, the internal history of rehearsal often contained scenes that were highly fraught. Naturally, attractions occurred that sometimes led to people leaving plays and in some cases, I'm sorry to say, led to serious marital breakdown. Because of course the whole business of rehearsal can be an extraordinarily difficult and tricky business, maybe because of the unusual emotions that are aroused or called for by particular roles. Human chemistry can lead to very tricky situations in the rather artificial, hothouse atmosphere of sustained rehearsal over a period of time. During rehearsals, you're out of the house for a month, from the perspective of the husband or wife or partner. Sadly, this cumulatively took its toll on the family life of some of our strongest and most committed members.

There is a very positive side to theatre work in that it can lead to social integration, maybe particularly for strangers. Elaine Stevens, one of our very best members and supports over the years, came to Cork from Wales and I think the entire theatre scene in Cork, of which she became a skilled and important part, served to make her almost more Cork than Cork people themselves. It integrated her and her delightful husband Alan into the community. Alan was a senior officer in the oil refinery at Whitegate and he was a great supporter and attender of all Elaine's activities, both in Everyman and in the musical comedies where she was always equally excellent.

By the mid to late 1980s there was talk of Everyman moving out of the Father Mathew Hall and buying the Palace.

One of the other problems with regard to the Father Mathew Hall was the retention of its use as a bingo hall on Sunday nights. This meant we did not have the Sunday nights, which made a difference in terms of 'get-outs' and 'get-ins' at weekends. The Capuchins found that their fund-raising needs required them to use the theatre

Ustinov's Everyman cast of Halfway Up the Tree. *l–r: Joss Cahill, Tony Callanan, Elaine Stevens, Eilis Geary, Dan Donovan, Pakey O'Callaghan and Melody McNamara.*

on a more regular basis. Our operation there was getting tight. Furthermore by the early 1980s we were also beginning to lose a little money, even with the Arts Council grants for the professional side of things. The possibility of undertaking the salvaging of the Palace for live theatre began to come onto our horizon. A firm in debt cannot buy a building. Our big asset was a house that had been left to us next to the Father Mathew Hall. It had been used for rehearsal space, a store and for board meetings. Since we had to be solvent to purchase a premises, we had to secure our total solvency by selling that house. This is where Leachlain's great heroic work began. A fairly long, Byzantine process of discussion between Leachlain and the other directors began. We continued at Father Mathew Hall, right into the late 1980s, having put down some ready cash with a very general agreement that we would very likely make a deal with Ward Anderson to take over the Palace. But finally, a very generous agreement was made with Ward Anderson who sold the Palace to us for £120,000, payable at £10,000 per annum. It was an act of extraordinary generosity to us and to the people of Cork.

When Ward Anderson closed the Palace cinema in 1988 did you all see an opportunity?

Like everything else, cinema was changing. The biggest proprietors of the film business in Ireland were Ward Anderson from Dublin. In Cork they owned the Capitol and the Palace cinemas. Cinema was going through a crisis of attendance, a cycle that does occur. The dire prophets of total destruction for the cinema were to prove inaccurate because cinema adapted to change. One of the ways it adapted was to provide a much bigger range of films in the cinemas. We have the rise of the cineplex. Ward Anderson decided to develop the Capitol Cineplex, leaving the future of the Palace from their point of view in great doubt. Dan Lowrey's music hall auditorium was, in a sense, becoming surplus to their requirements. The fact that the auditorium was listed put considerable difficulty in the way of doing anything drastic with the old building, which in any case was not in good repair. The process was a very slow one. It was a time of change for both groups: for Ward Anderson and for Everyman.

Not every one of our directors agreed with a policy of moving to the Palace. In fairness to him, Michael McCarthy felt that it was too big, too dilapidated and that any effort to use it would frustrate the policy of Everyman. There was a good deal of truth in that view. We moved from the small scale of CYMS to the medium scale of Father Mathew and now there is a giant leap into a different ball game altogether, a 900-seater, old-fashioned theatre, not adapted to the needs of our productions. The saving of the Palace for Cork was not necessarily furthering the real aims of Everyman as it had developed over the years.

The Everyman Palace Theatre, Cork, c. *2005.*

However, there were reasons other than the re-housing of Everyman and the saving of the Palace for future Cork audiences that induced us to follow up the possibility of acquiring the Palace building on 15 MacCurtain Street, formerly King Street. Of course there was the tradition of the old Dan Lowrey music hall which long preceded the use of the Palace as theatre or cinema. From a personal angle there were the years of exile while the Opera House was being rebuilt, when the Cork Operatic Society was welcomed very warmly to the Palace, a kind of a substitute home.

Your memories of the Palace as a theatre go way back?

I can recall a post-war production of *Othello* by the Loft one Sunday afternoon there. I think Seán Clayton, a CEO with a VEC up country, played Othello. The VEC system at its best was a strong influence in sustaining cultural activity at a time when there were very few structured organisations to provide training and involvement in the arts. I always remember their generosity in giving me a drama class at the School of Music, to help Compántas Chorcaí in the training and rehearsal of plays, particularly Seán Ó Tuama's. Pilib Ó Laoghaire, director of Cór Cois Laoi, would have a VEC background. The present director of the Cork International Choral Festival, John Fitzpatrick, is regularly employed by Cork VEC and is seconded as director to the International Choral Festival. All down the years the VEC supported local cultural activities and they did not interpret their brief over-rigidly.

The bar was always fairly important in the many lives of the Palace. When Billy Ahern was manager there, it was a warm watering hole with a very regular and somewhat mature clientele. Billy was a genial man who would enjoy a little tipple when the night's performance was over. It is alleged that one night when he was making his weary way home in the early hours of the morning, he was accosted by one of the ladies of the night in Parnell Place. He dismissed her rather contemptuously with the words 'Run along, little girl, I'm in the entertainment business myself.'

To retain the bar licence, which was a theatre licence, there were always some stage shows mounted in the Palace, so when it became a cinema under the Ward Anderson regime it remained in atmosphere something more of a theatre than a cinema. Der Breen succeeded Billy. Der's own work in Cork theatre in the 1940s and 1950s led to a very theatrical atmosphere in the Palace bar, which was done up during his regime. It became highly popular, particularly with members of the Cork Film Society. The strength of that lies behind the institution of the Film Festival in 1956. Several nights of the week you might find maybe Máighréad Murphy, who did tremendous work on the committee of the Film Society for many years and her husband Séamus,[42] who was of course taught by Corkery. Máighréad's father, Joseph Higgins, the sculptor from Youghal who died young, had done portrait busts of Corkery and Stockley. It was Fleischmann

Daniel Corkery and his portrait bust by Joseph Higgins.

who persuaded Alfie O'Rahilly to have the bust of Corkery cast in bronze and that's why it's in the University. Curiously, Máighréad and Séamus lived in the house that had been the home of the older Fleischmanns. Máighréad still lives there.[43]

I had the honour of doing the soundtrack for Louis Marcus's film on Séamus, *The Silent Art* (1959). It was written by Louis to footage that he filmed. He made an extraordinarily living picture of Séamus at work over quite a wide range of activities. Páidí Collins who used to teach in Christians was another regular in the Palace bar. Bob Breathnach, my lecturer in UCC, who many years later brought me back to the English Department as a tutor and maybe Seán Hendrick as chairman of the Cork Film Club might be there. Seán Ó Ríordáin the poet would often drop in. John A. Murphy might be there as well. Discussions were sometimes very lively. Geraldine Neeson, although living quite near, would not be likely to frequent the bar. Of course Daniel Corkery would be *most* unlikely to visit a licensed premises.

By the time he died in 1975, Séamus had carved the gravestones for many of the people we have been discussing: Corkery, Seán Neeson and Anew McMaster all went to their eternal reward in the

1960s. After he came back from Paris in the early 1930s, the head-stones helped Séamus through hard physical slog to make a living as an artist based in Cork. Inspiration and perspiration were combined to do that, at a time when commissions for artists were very scarce. Corkery had helped his former national school pupil secure the Gibson scholarship to go to Paris.

Tell me more about the role the Arts Council played in helping acquire the Palace.

We informed the Arts Council of the possibility of getting the Palace, refurbishing it and transferring our operation there. At a superficial level it looked as though this was overall a good thing. But the problems were enormous. The Arts Council, who were not totally in charge of capital funding, felt that the costs might be too high. They offered us their usual help and co-operation. We had a good rapport with Phelim Donlon, who dealt with theatre. Donn McMullin and Brian Bolingbroke, one of our directors, went to government to ascertain whether finance could be sought from European Structural Funds. At that stage, Anthony Cronin[44] was optimistic that help could be obtained. We lobbied all the political parties, and all our Cork TDs. Somehow or other a large tranche of money from official sources had to be obtained. We found a general enthusiasm for the whole operation of saving the Palace for Cork. I think we blinded ourselves a little with a touch of inadequately supported optimism. We had started to do a little groundwork locally to develop a fund-raising campaign. Our own fund-raising had to be reinforced. This campaign was based on the needs of the city and the existence of this historic building, which was to be refurbished as a centre of excellence for theatre. Locally, Peter Barry kick-started the campaign with an extremely generous contribution. Peter became involved with a body of trustees who would keep an eye on the overall refurbishment.

Little did we know that the decision to go ahead would cause a fateful discontinuity in our practical theatrical activities. Suddenly we came to a full stop. The Father Mathew Hall was more or less over for us. The Arts Council were still insistent that any subsidy they gave us would be applied strictly to the professional aspects of the theatre. We had pragmatically worked our little enterprise over the years in terms of keeping a constant supply of plays on the stage, as they became available. The question of whether the thing was professional or not formed little part of our concern. We had started as a community with few resources and were used to operating on a kind of independent level. Indirect subsidies were provided by the unpaid work of a large body of willing volunteers both on and off stage. Among the veterans of this group is Maureen O'Keefe, who has looked after the front of house sweet-shop which contributed and continues to contribute in a very practical way to keeping the enterprise solvent and on the road. People like Brendan Casserly have contributed hugely. He and other volunteers are always there, a welcoming presence that personalise the theatre.

Time passed while we wrestled with the problem. The wear and tear on personnel was at times enormous. One of the solutions had to be to try and trade ourselves out of the difficulties by getting the doors open, somehow or other. Various tasks were undertaken and eventually the theatre was in a state where it could open in 1990. Cork Corporation were as generous as circumstances at the time allowed. It was costing an arm and a leg to put on a show there, never mind refurbishment. The old amateur idea was beginning to fail. People wanted to be paid. Any money we raised went on hand-to-mouth requirements. Inflation was running high. Hence the hike in expenses. The Arts Council were happy with the Everyman programmes over the years but perhaps failed to realise that this was all made possible by the sacrifices of the founders, organisers and volunteers. I can recall numerous visits to the AIB in South Mall, getting them to continue to back us up, despite a rather depressing prognosis. Dan Lowrey's music hall was unfortunately rather jerry-built, with a roof of contrasting bits of materials here and there. Our Irish climate sometimes made its presence felt on our cash customers sitting in the stalls. My attention was now on administration. I had ceased to be active in the practical and creative work of Everyman. My principal performance was a kind of public pretence that all was well with the Palace. It was a fairly good piece of acting, because our situation was really dire.

Morale was low in all those aware of the inherent snags. The problem increasingly came to affect the health of the management. There was an increasing sense that we had drawn an intractable problem on ourselves. Two of the major shareholders were ill at one time. Donn's departure as general manager was a further serious blow to the company's morale and the appointment of a successor without a public advertisement led almost to a breakdown in our relations with the Arts Council. They were unhappy with Donn's replacement and they made their feelings very clear. The appointment, with the Arts Council's approval, of Vincent O'Shea led to our running grants being maintained. The salaries of our professional staff were secured.

Through the good offices of Dick Langford, then CEO of the City of Cork VEC, I had an interview with the director of the Arts Council, Adrian Munnelly, one Saturday afternoon in Limerick. He gave me considerable help in plotting a way through and out of our troubles. But in fact there was light at the end of the tunnel. One of our board members, Toddy O'Sullivan, became a Minister of State in the mid 1990s. Wonderful to relate, this government also had a minister, Michael D. Higgins, whose brief was the Arts. A further tranche of European Structural Funding was on the horizon and this time, thanks to the good offices of Toddy and Michael D., we secured a substantial amount of funding. We thought we had blown the entire thing, because we heard that Michael D. had come to Cork and visited the theatre without speaking to any of the directors or our trusty chairman, Michael White. He rambled into the auditorium and throughout the building, doing his own reconnaissance. Monica Spencer was the artistic director and contributed mightily at this important and crucial stage. It marked the start of our revival and redevelopment.

It was a great achievement to save the Palace, if exhausting for everyone involved. How did you relax?

One of the weekly consolations that I managed to preserve throughout these difficult times was my Sunday visits to the countryside with the Riverstown Foot Beagling Club. That covered the area over the hills and vales of Glanmire, from Sarsfield Court right across the country to Knockraha, visiting each meet twice a year. The Club had a great democratic mix in which all ages and all classes participated. There was a delightful sense of companionship and while many people might have reservations about blood sports, the old timers were very strict on the principle of giving the hare the 'Law'. As a matter of fact the hunt rather than the kill was primary. There were great beagling families, the Dalys, the Lambes, the O'Callaghans and many others, who kept hounds and had a traditional input into the sport for decades. The variety of scene, the fresh air and the good fellowship made Sundays very relaxing. Not least was the aftermath of the hunt. It always happened that the hunters retired to the nearest local, usually the Castle Tavern, where our hosts Lil and Michael Canavan welcomed us and on special days provided us with great bowls of crubeens. After a few drinks, as was customary with all sporting clubs at the time, the music began. There were always a few hounds in the Tavern sharing the celebrations with their masters. A very popular figure in the beagling world and beyond was Mick McCarthy, whose skills as a maker of hurleys were deeply appreciated down the years by so many Cork hurlers.

Among the many other members who rejoiced our hearts and our ears over the years was Paddy Kiely, a former worker with Murphy's Brewery, a large, amiable man with a splendid tenor voice. In those days the licensing laws caused the festivities to end at seven o'clock and though we stretched it out a bit, it became necessary for Michael Canavan to clear the house,

Veterans of Riverstown Foot Beagles, Paddy Kiely and Mick McCarthy.

which by that time would be really swinging. I remember Paddy beginning *In Bodenstown Churchyard*, the song about Wolfe Tone, on one occasion. The proprietor raised his eyes to heaven, saying 'We'll be here for the night: there are about 50 verses to that.' All that is now a vanished world.

But I remember the saving of the Palace as one of the most painful and laborious phases of my life, where I was caught in an administrative bind that sat ill with my temperament.

Could you see the 1980s as a period of consolidation in relation to Pres?

I was seriously cutting down my theatre workload in the 1980s. In 1981 I had some warnings about overdoing it. [Dr] Con Murphy was concerned. I was hospitalised that February for the first time in my life. My consultant, Professor Denis O'Sullivan, was a class ahead of me in Pres. Like myself he had a country background and also came from a teaching background. His mother was a teacher in Dripsey, I think, and was a good friend of my own mother's. He was a brilliant student in Pres and followed his school career with a marvellous history of subsequent work and research, which culminated in his becoming dean of the faculty of medicine in UCC. He has written a book[45] on the history of the medical faculty in UCC. He too loves to sail. At any rate he found me in the Regional Hospital in Bishopstown and having captured me in his fortress, subjected me to every test that he could think of. He was an expert in diabetes. The import of what he said was that it would be advisable to reduce my workload. I did have chest pains but it seemed they were more diabetes-related than coronary-related. The worst news was that he felt that it desirable that I should reduce my weight from 14 stone 8 ounces to 12 stone. This began one of the toughest regimes of my life. For about six months I fought the hard battle until eventually I shed the flab. The six-month sentence included not touching a drink. I ended up slim, trim and brimful of energy and have ever since been careful to keep my weight at the proper level. This meant a more controlled lifestyle.

As a teacher I was an excellent attender at school. I rarely missed a day. When I returned to Pres, pale and lacking in energy, Brother Jerome was the heart and soul of kindness to me. I was his deputy headmaster at the time. The promotion system which existed in the national schools had been brought into play during the re-organisation of secondary schools in the early 1970s. In the context of schools run by religious orders, there were now promotion opportunities for lay teachers to become deputies to the religious leaders. Freddie Holland my old teacher, a fine mathematician who also taught in UCC, became the first vice-principal. I succeeded him and became vice-principal for fifteen years. I was teaching all the time, doing about ten hours a week, half the usual amount and would continue to do so until I retired in 1991. To tell the truth, I liked the classroom and was less than enamoured by some of the tedious administrative tasks I had to undertake as vice-principal. When you are kicked upstairs in education you can find the administration demanding but dull.

The renaissance of Pres came when Brother Jerome came home from the West Indies to a meeting of the Chapter of the Order, where he was elected as one of the Assistant Superior Generals and allotted to Pres. Pres was always administered by one of the Assistant Generals of the Order because of its being adjacent to Mount St Joseph in Blarney Street, where they had their headquarters. The Presentation contribution to Cork was always very significant. Apart from Pres they originally held the South Monastery adjacent to the famous girls' school where my aunt Kit taught. They had their junior school in Scoil Mhuire on the Douglas Road. There were facilities in Mount St Joseph for training brothers. They subsequently established the well-known schools at Turner's Cross and Spioraid Naofa in Bishopstown.

Before Jerome's arrival, Pres had gone into rather a slide. It needed fresh administrative update. Jerome was one of the many Presentation Brothers who had done tremendous work in the West Indies in the founding of colleges and the training of personnel. Those colleges would have been based on the British colonial system. Jerome brought a totally new view to Pres based on those experiences and immediately began by taking a root-and-branch look at the structures prevailing in Pres. Free education had come in the late 1960s and Jerome was able to capitalise on the changes this brought. Not only did he gradually expand the curriculum but he also established a system of school prefects elected by the boys themselves. He invested in and developed media studies in a big way. He is of course most famous for the establishment of the SHARE organisation for providing housing for the poor.

What was the thinking there?

Increasingly, the exam system was focusing on the results of Inter and Leaving Cert exams. Pres had a strong allegiance to the old university matriculation system, which created space for extra-curricular activities. Increasingly, change was found to be desirable and led to the Transition year concept, taking at least some of the extreme concentration away from the old academic priorities. The establishment of SHARE necessitated a move away from the old authoritarian system and generated a trust in, and wider use of, the skills and talents of pupils in a much more libertarian atmosphere. With creative planning, the boys themselves had to take a substantial amount of responsibility in the establishing of SHARE. They visited old people, organised the Christmas fast, collected money and contacted the girls' schools to collect the money as well. The work of SHARE got rid of a whole lot of remaining bad housing. Some of the worst conditions have disappeared. The boys were brought, through this work, in creative and appropriate touch with Cork City Hall. Joe McHugh, the City Manager in the 1980s, became a great friend of Jerome's. His sons came to Pres when he was appointed to Cork and were members of the early SHARE committees. A huge number of the students became active from then on in the social and cultural affairs of the city.

1985 was a special year for Cork and for Pres in particular.

When I recovered my health, I continued my work with Everyman, though with a lesser personal input. When 1985 approached it was felt that some special events should be organised to mark the occasion of the eight hundreth anniversary of the granting of a charter to Cork City. An unexpected opportunity presented itself when Dean Maurice Carey of St Fin Barre's Cathedral approached me with the suggestion that in collaboration with Cork theatre in general, we might mount a production to mark this special event. We found that a very old friend of mine, Sam McCutcheon, vice-principal of Ashton, had been at work on the script of a historical pageant tracing some of the notable incidents in Cork's history, largely but not totally based on the Cathedral site itself. He showed me the script as written and sketched out the ideas he had for its expansion into a complete production in St Fin Barre's. A good deal of work was put in by the Cathedral authorities, particularly Dean Carey himself. Colin Nicholl had just come to Cork as Cathedral organist and helped with putting together ideas for the effective linkage of various episodes, through the appropriate choices of music, all put on tape. A complete committee under Marjorie Fitzmaurice, a very cultured woman particularly interested in costume, was put together. It was essential that the costumes be top class and be appropriate to their period. There had been a similar pageant some years before but because of the occasion, this production had to be done on a civic scale. Gathering a cast proved unexpectedly easy. Lots of my old colleagues of a lifetime rallied round and, though I didn't realise it at the time, it was to prove my swansong in the active life of Cork theatre production.

The Cork 800 celebrations were, I suppose, putting a brave face on a difficult period in Cork's economic history.

The 1980s were a bad time and this was felt in theatre as it was

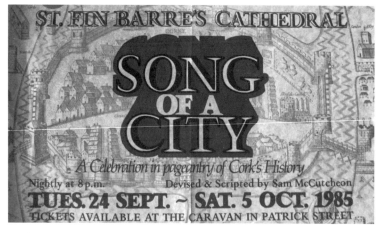

Cork 800 poster.

in many sectors. Everyman was in the height of trouble, with high inflation and problems about its venue. Costs of productions multiplied. TV was bringing big changes in support for theatre and it seemed a watershed in the history of Cork show business. There was a sense of betrayal in regard to Joan Denise Moriarty. Her funding was dramatically withdrawn after 40 years of work. Jack Lynch had gone. He had made the positive gesture when her star was high. Frankly, the treatment of her was I thought largely through envy. The Ballet Company and all her teaching were damaged. For whose good? Taking her off the scene served nobody. She became dependent on the generosity of her friends, because her life's work in dance and music was so selfless, so physically wrenching on her system and she so dedicated to it, that she never really made arrangements for shelter and care in later life. Single women of her generation did not often buy houses. They lived in digs or flats. Hence Betty's worry that I might walk out some morning and shut the door here behind me.

Cork's economy, with the closing of the Ford and Dunlop plants in the city and the closing of the textile factories at Dripsey, Blarney,

Douglas and Blackpool, was coming into serious crisis. The general prosperity that Cork took for granted, while much of Ireland suffered deprivation, was now collapsing.

Another of the challenges at this demanding time was that the old Pres buildings on the Western Road, which had served well since 1887 or 8, were now inadequate and really required total modernisation. When the task was confronted and studied it was felt that perhaps a total rebuilding on the green field across the road might be a better solution than fiddling around with changes on an inadequate site. The sports complex at Wilton now proved to have been a most significant development.

During Jerome's last years, much investment went into the problem of the future of the College on its existing site. However before matters were fully decided, as is the way with religious orders, Brother Jerome was elected Superior General and had to leave Pres. Luckily he was succeeded by a Brother who had down the years got experience as a builder of schools, Brother Bartholomew, known affectionately in the Order as Bart the Builder. He was in charge of the school during the five-year period when the plans were finally drawn up and all our resources were devoted to putting a worthy building on the ample site provided by the old playing fields across the banks of the River Lee. The next five years of my life, which half explains why I had to limit my theatre work, were concentrated fairly strongly on the planning and preparation for all of these fundamental changes. Bartholomew's health was unfortunately failing but he soldiered on with great enthusiasm. Our sights were looking towards a new and exciting horizon, so that part of the old Cork tradition and the strong historical input of the Presentation Brothers could be expanded and continued. It was a great thrill to be part of this endeavour. The new school was opened in 1985. I had my final sixth year cycle in the new school, teaching and administering in it from 1985 until 1991.

A few years before my retirement, Betty got a sudden violent attack of arthritis. Blair's Pharmacy on 7 St Patrick's Street closed, causing her and the rest of the staff great shock. It was one of the oldest pharmacies on Patrick Street, going back to the nineteenth century when a Scottish grandfather of Mr Gordon Blair opened it. What was thought of as a temporary problem with Betty's health became seriously chronic and permanent. Ulcers developed. There followed a ten-year decline until her death in 1996, by which time both her legs had been amputated. I was very taken up with her suffering and left in despair about the steady decline of her health. In all this I was wonderfully helped beyond the call of duty by all her old colleagues in Blair's. Both my sisters were in fact failing but Betty required constant care. Patty was in one sense the survivor. She lived as long as she could and then she died. She got a stroke on the August Bank holiday of 1994 and died in hospital two months later. She had been operating on her own in her flat in Dunmanway right up to the stroke. She was 84 when she died.

I had dreams of retirement. I would be free to do all the things I hadn't done. I had a particular little dream of visiting lots of islands, not just Irish ones but Scottish ones. When Betty started needing my almost constant care, I was glad of the fulfillment I had during my working years, teaching, doing so many plays and getting stuck into so many things.

I was talking to John O'Shea about the whole Everyman business the other day. We were saying that things often run in twenty-year cycles. Presentation Theatre Guild, Compántas, even Everyman could be said to have had twenty-year cycles. The careless rapture cannot last. Maybe staleness sets in. John wondered had we been inhibitory. Had we held the high ground when it was no longer as fresh as it had been? It is in the cyclical nature of things that other endeavours should replace ours. 'The old order changeth, giving way to new.'

Notes

1. Interviewed in Cork on 10, 24, January; 9, 15, 23, 30 March; 27 April; 16, 25 May; 9, 14, 15, 22 June; 6, 10, 12, 13, 18, 19, 25, 26 July; 21, 28 August; 5, 18, September 2007.
2. Tomás Ó Canainn, *Seán Ó Riada His Life and Work* (The Collins Press, Cork, 2003).
3. Shane O'Toole, *Faith restored in Barry Byrne's vision* (Archiseek, 2002).
4. Seamus Murphy, *Stone Mad* (Golden Eagle Publications, Dublin, 1950) p. ix.
5. Thanks to Professor Brendan O'Mahony and Fr Dermot Lynch at Holy Trinity Church.
6. John A. Murphy, *The College A History of University/Queen's College Cork* (Cork University Press, Cork, 1995).
7. See Sean Dunne (ed.), *The Cork Anthology* (Cork University Press, Cork, 1993) for a selection of writings by some of the people discussed in this chapter.
8. Ruth Fleischmann (ed.), *Aloys Fleischmann (1910–1992) A Life For Music in Ireland Remembered by Contemporaries* (Mercier Press, Cork and Dublin, 2000).
9. Seamas de Barra, *Aloys Fleischmann* (Field Day, 2006).
10. Ruth Fleischmann (ed.), *Joan Denise Moriarty Founder of the Irish National Ballet: Material for a History of Dance in Ireland* (Mercier Press, Cork and Dublin, 1998), pp. 126–129.
11. See Maurice Harmon's *Sean O'Faolain A Life* (Constable, London, 1994), and *Sean O'Faolain A Critical Introduction* (Wolfhound Press, Dublin, 1984).
12. B. G. MacCarthy, *Women Writers: Their Contribution to the English Novel 1621–1744* and *The Later Women Novelists 1744–1818* (Blackwell, Oxford, 1947) and *The Female Pen: Women Writers and Novelists 1621–1818* (Cork University Press, Cork, 1999).
13. Declan Kiberd, *Inventing Ireland The Literature of the Modern Nation* (Vintage, 1996) p. 558.
14. Paul Delaney, 'Fierce Passions for Middle Aged Men. Frank O'Connor and Daniel Corkery' in Hilary Lennon (ed.), *Frank O'Connor Critical Essays* (Four Courts Press, Dublin, 2007).
15. James Matthews, *Voices A Life of Frank O'Connor* (Gill & Macmillan, Dublin, 1983).
16. Patrick Maume, '*Life that is exile': Daniel Corkery and the search for Irish Ireland* (Institute of Irish Studies, Belfast, 1993). Includes a full bibliography of Corkery's work.
17. Dan Donovan in Ruth Fleischmann (ed.), *Joan Denise Moriarty Founder of Irish National Ballet: Material for a History of Dance in Ireland* (Mercier Press, Cork and Dublin, 1998), pp. 126–129.
18. Colin Rynne, Billy Wigham, *Forgotten Cork: Photographs from the Day Collection* (The Collins Press, Cork, 2005).
19. Dan Donovan, 'The Presentation Theatre Guild', *Presentation Brothers College Cork 1887–1954 Extension Souvenir* (ed.), Rev Br Austin, pp. 134–139.
20. Geraldine Neeson, '*In my Mind's Eye' The Cork I Knew and Loved* (Prestige Books, Dublin, 2001).

21. James Matthews, *op. cit.*, pp. 52–3.

22. Christopher Fitz-Simon, *The Boys: A Biography of Micheál Mac Liammóir and Hilton Edwards* (Nick Hearn, London, 1994), pp 49–50.

23. Robert Welch, *The Abbey Theatre 1899–1999 Form and Pressure* (Oxford University Press, Oxford, 1999).

24. Lennox Robinson (ed.), *The Journals of Lady Gregory 1916–1930* (Macmillan New York, New York,1947).

25. B. G. MacCarthy, *The Whip Hand* (Duffy, Dublin, 1943).

26. Michael O'Connor, *Just Billa* (The Mercier Press, Cork and Dublin, 2000), p. 113.

27. Daniel Corkery was appointed a member of the first Arts Council in 1951, on the recommendation of P. J. Little, director.

28. On Wednesday 29 May 1957 *The Cork Evening Press* carried a full page on the play with nine rehearsal photos.

29. See for example Seán Ó Tuama's *Repossessions* (Cork University Press, Cork, 1995) for insight into his prose work in English and Irish.

30. Catherine Candy, *Priestly Fictions* (Wolfhound Press, Dublin, 1995).

31. Alberto Degiacomo, *TC Murray, Dramatist – Voice of The Irish Peasant* (Syracuse University Press, 2002).

32. Dan Donovan in Ruth Fleischmann (ed.), *Cork International Choral Festival 1954–2004 A Celebration* (Glen House Press, Germany), pp. 368–372.

33. John McSweeney, *The Golden Age of Cork Cinemas* (Rose Arch Publications, 2003).

34. Rockett in Kevin Rockett, Luke Gibbons, John Hill (eds.), *Cinema and Ireland* (Syracuse University Press, 1988), pp. 86, 110.

35. Gus Smith and Des Hickey, *John B The Real Keane* (Mercier Press, Cork and Dublin, 1992), pp. 87-91; John B. Keane, *Self Portrait* (Mercier Press, Cork and Dublin, 1969).

36. Merlin Waterson, *The Servants' Hall A Domestic History of Erddig* (Routledge, London 1980).

37. Watters & Murtagh, *Infinite Variety Dan Lowrey's Music Hall 1879–97* (Gill & Macmillan, Dublin, 1975).

38. Brigitte Le Juez Beckett, *Avant la Lettre* (Bernard Grasset, Paris, 2007).

39. In 1967 legislation abolished the permanent ban on certain books, releasing all books banned before 1955, which amounted to 5,000 titles.

40. Arthur Miller, *Timebends* (Grove, New York, 1987).

41. B. G. MacCarthy, *The Psychology of Genius: Studies in Browning* (University of London Press, London, 1936).

42. Crawford Art Gallery, *Séamus Murphy 1907–1975 Sculptor* (Gandon Editions, Kinsale, 2007).

43. Máighréad Murphy in Ruth Fleischmann (ed.), *Aloys Fleischmann (1910–1992) A Life for Music in Ireland Remembered by Contemporaries* (Mercier Press, Cork and Dublin, 2000), pp. 360–363.

44. Writer and, for a time, Arts adviser to C. J. Haughey.

45. Denis J. O'Sullivan, *The Cork School of Medicine A History* (University College Cork, Cork, 2007).

Index